The Master

The Rev. Dr. Sheldon MacKenzie ... preacher. He loves the Lord Jesus and His teaching. He enjoyed sharing that story with others in classes, sermons, talks, conversations, and in his many books. I especially commend him for his recent books on the Gospels. They tell us who Jesus was and is and what Christian discipleship means. They are excellent resource material for students, preaching, Bible study groups, personal reflection, and for those searching for direction in living. Anyone will feel better after reading one of Sheldon's books.
    The Right Rev. Mark Genge, D.D.
    Retired Anglican Bishop

Dr. MacKenzie speaks of this book as "an attempt to be faithful both to the first readers and hearers of the Gospel of John and to those who read and hear it proclaimed today." He has done that very successfully and clearly as he examines twenty-five selections from John's Gospel. While other Gospel writers tell of Jesus' life and ministry, John's sermons, in a unique way, point us to Jesus as the Christ. An example of this is shown in the ninth chapter of John as Jesus gave sight to the man born blind ... It is the confession of faith (by the man formerly blind) in Jesus as Lord that is carried throughout John's Gospel. Dr. MacKenzie, in his very scholarly yet personal style of writing, lets John The Master Preacher bring the Good News of the first century to us in the twenty-first.
    The Rev. Donald Stroh
    Lutheran Pastor, Retired

The author of this book, The Rev. Dr. R. Sheldon MacKenzie, is a biblical scholar and preacher. He has experience in the parish ministry as well as being a university professor. These experiences, together with his studies and faith, are the background for the twenty-five excellent sermons on John's Gospel contained in this book. As an added bonus, he writes in the language and style of a poet ...

It is clear throughout the book that the writer presents his Gospel and, in the process, constructs his dialogues with an open-endedness that makes evident the immediate truth which the text conveys, as well as its equally important deeper spiritual meaning, for then as for now. ... The tensions between the Church and Synagogue when this Gospel was written (late first century AD) are clear. Dr. MacKenzie notes that the word Jew *is "used in John to indicate unbelievers (p. 79)," and is not intended to convey any anti-Semitic bias.*

This book is a great resource for the preacher as well as for Bible-study groups. It has an excellent bibliography. I recommend it highly both to the novice and the seasoned student of Saint John's Gospel.
        The Rev. Dr. Canon Frank Cluett
        Retired Provost, Queen's Theological College

The Master Preacher *is a welcome addition to Dr. MacKenzie's previous publications and represents a distinct contribution to literature in the field of Homiletics by a Canadian preacher. Dr. MacKenzie, through his careful and thorough exegetical and hermeneutical work on the readings from John's Gospel on which these sermons are based, draws out their meaning with insight and imagination. The sermons are written in a clear, vivid, and engaging style and this adds to the appeal of* The Master Preacher.
        The Rev. Dr. Morley F. Hodder
        Emeritus Professor, Department of Religious Studies
        Memorial University, St. John's, Newfoundland

In his book, Credo, *William Sloane Coffin, former minister of Riverside Church, New York City, states, "Good preaching is never at* people; *it's* for *people. ... Good preaching raises to a conscious level of knowledge inherent in everyone's experience of life. It tells people what in their heart of hearts they already know, what in the depth of their souls they are only waiting to hear confirmed...." On the basis of that definition this recent book of sermons by Dr.*

MacKenzie is truly good preaching. ... These sermons are excellent examples in dealing with the life experiences of ordinary people. They help us to see ourselves as subjects in these stories. At the same time, they shed new light on the Gospel texts on which they are built. These sermons reveal Jesus' presence in the lives of ordinary people bringing meaning and redemption to their existence.

    The Rev. Dr. J. Kenneth MacLeod
    Minister, The Presbyterian Church in Canada
    Retired

The Master Preacher: Sermons From John, *reminds us again that John's Gospel uses words and ideas unique to itself. In the author's words, "it is more an interpretation of Jesus Christ than it is an account of his life and ministry that we find in Matthew, Mark, and Luke." The sermons, devotions found therein are as preached with the skill of a poet and enriched by his academic and pastoral heart. I read his* Joy To The World, God Was In Christ, *and* The Face Of Christmas *and found myself thinking "what seeds for a Christmas meditation!" As we move through John's Gospel with words giving flesh to such meaningful titles as "Wine For The Wedding," "When Religion Got Involved," "The One With The Crook," to "The Heart Of The Gospel." With a diversity of subject matter we are drawn forward until amongst the author's last words in "The Man From Nazareth" we are met by God in terms of human life.*

    The Rev. Dr. Douglas MacEachern
    Past Professor — Nova Scotia Agricultural College
    Retired Minister, The United Church of Canada
    The above appeared in a Newsletter to
        United Church Clergy in New Brunswick

... there is always something lost when a sermon is brought to the printed page. Like a play, or perhaps more specifically like a great soliloquy within the play, the words carry layers of meaning of nuance and inflection when heard rather than read. The remarkable thing about the published sermons of Dr. MacKenzie is not merely (merely! ... a weak word for an increasing rarity) a

unique voice, but also how little of that voice is lost from pulpit to print.

I have been privileged to hear Dr. MacKenzie in person, over many years as have had many others on the numerous occasions when he has been asked to preach or to address assemblies "grander" than a humble and ordinary Sunday morning service — a distinction he would emphatically dismiss. That gives me an advantage, no doubt, but in the way the sermons in this volume (and his other collections) appear on the page — very like lines from a play — the rhythms and cadence of his voice from pulpit or podium are conveyed as close to a recording as the printed word can get.

He eschews polysyllabic words like "eschew" and "polysyllabic," using a simple and direct vocabulary that nevertheless betrays years of New Testament scholarship and teaching at Memorial University. His intimate knowledge of the Greek text and the work of other scholar-commentators never intrudes in a disruptive or obvious way.

No less than five of the sermons come from chapter nine — the story of the man born blind and the hullabaloo of nastiness after he had been given his sight by Jesus. I confess that at first I was a little fatigued with such a concentration, anxious to get on with fresh settings. It is only by reading them through that, at the end, you see why Dr. MacKenzie has spend so much time and space on the story, perhaps itself originally a sermon!

    The Rev. Dr. James R. Dickey
    Minister, St. Paul's Presbyterian Church
    Hamilton, Ontario
    Past Editor, *The Presbyterian Record*

The Master Teacher
Sermons From Mark

Roy Sheldon MacKenzie

Fairway Press
Lima, Ohio

THE MASTER TEACHER

*In memory of my parents
Harold and Gladys MacKenzie
who loved both the Lord of the Church
and the Church itself*

FIRST EDITION
Copyright © 2007 by
Roy Sheldon MacKenzie

All rights reserved. No portion of this book may be reproduced or utilized in any form or by any means, electronic or mechanical including photocopying, without permission in writing from the publisher. Inquiries should be addressed to: Sheldon MacKenzie, 129-6001 Promontory Road, Chilliwack, British Columbia V2R 3E3.

Library Of Congress Control Number: 2007935331

ISBN 10: 0-7880-2189-3
ISBN 13: 978-0-7880-2189-3

PRINTED IN U.S.A.

Other Titles By Sheldon MacKenzie

The Passion According To John

The Words He Spoke

The Isolated Jesus

Gathered By The River:
A History of the West River Seminary and Theological Hall (1848-1858)

The Power And The Glory (Mark 8, 9, 10)

The Master Story Teller: Sermons From Luke

The Master Preacher: Sermons From John

Introduction

When Paul wrote to the churches with which he was concerned
> and when he wrote to Philemon, the slave owner,
>> he used as his model the secular letter.

The main difference
> between a secular letter of the first century
>> and a letter from Paul was the content of the letters.

As a form of writing it was not new or original.

When Mark wrote his Gospel
> he was doing something no one before him had done.

As far as we know
> no one had ever written a Gospel.

A Gospel is a form of writing unique to Christian people.

Other people wrote letters, histories, biographies, or diaries.
> No other people wrote Gospels.

The Gospels of Matthew, Mark, and Luke are remarkably alike.

They are called the Synoptic Gospels. *provide a general summary -*

They are called the Synoptic Gospels
> because if set side by side they can be read together.

They tell much the same story in the same way.

They look at the same things from a similar point of view.

The Synoptic Gospels
> belong to what is called the synoptic tradition.

The synoptic tradition means that they make use
> of similar traditional material about Jesus.

This similar traditional material
> had been circulating in the primitive Christian communities.

This traditional material would consist
> a) of sayings *of* Jesus
> b) and stories *about* Jesus
>> that had come to be the common property of the early church.

When this material was written down,
> as it is in the Synoptic Gospels,
>> it took the *form* of direct sayings of Jesus.

It took an almost reporter style *form* of stories *about* Jesus.
This is an important feature to remember.
The stories and sayings took the *form* of direct sayings
    and the *form* of documentary reporting.
Today we are told by the foremost biblical scholars
    that many of the sayings of Jesus
        and much of the story material had already been used
            and passed on by Christian preachers, prophets, and
                teachers.
Secondly,
    we know now that many of the sayings and stories
        that have come down to us in the Synoptic Gospels
            reflect the interests and concerns of the churches
                in which they were used.
One of the remarkable features of the early Church
    is precisely this one — that the Church taught its members
        in the *form* of the sayings of Jesus
        and through stories about him.
In this way each Gospel is a reflection of two situations:
    a) the situation of its own particular community, and
    b) the actual situation in which Jesus taught.
This is what Mark has done.
He speaks to the Church in his own day
    "in the form of a story of Jesus teaching his disciples."
For example,
    when Mark is dealing with the problems of discipleship
        in the church at Rome, for which he is writing,
            he does so in the form of a story about Jesus and Peter.
You see, at one and the same time,
    Mark telling a story about Jesus and Peter,
        and also about the Risen Lord and the Christian disciple
            of the time at which he is writing.
At any time in the Gospel of Mark
    when you hear Jesus addressing the disciples in Galilee
        you are also hearing Jesus speaking
            to the members of the Church for which Mark is
                writing.

In this Gospel the past, present, and future all flow together.
There is the past of the ministry of Jesus in Galilee.
There is the present of the ministry of the risen Jesus
   in the Church.
And there is the future ministry,
   which Jesus will exercise when he comes again as Son of Man.
The past, present, and future all flow together in this Gospel.
A reader may miss the present and future aspects in Mark
   and stick to the past — as many have done and do.
That is called exegesis without hermeneutics.
If you do that
   you will miss a good bit of what the evangelist
      is trying to get across to his readers and hearers.
One of the themes in Mark's Gospel is a characteristic
   of the disciples.
They consistently misunderstand what Jesus is saying
   and doing.
They see but do not see! They hear and do not hear!
This theme follows through
   from the first chapter until the last.
The Gospel of Mark is the shortest of the Synoptic Gospels.
You may read it in a few hours.
         I hope you will!

[handwritten: exegesis — an explanation on the meaning of a text]

[handwritten: hermeneutics — interpreting]

Table Of Contents

1. A Wild Man In A Muddy River 13
   Mark 1:1-11

2. Aprons And Fig Leaves 19
   Mark 1:12-13

3. A Visible Sign 27
   Mark 2:1-12

4. Lord Of The Flies 35
   Mark 3:13-15, 19b-30

5. Mistaken Identity! 41
   Mark 3:19b-30

6. You Are Family! 47
   Mark 3:26-35

7. A Model For Mission 53
   Mark 4:1-9

8. What Time Is It? 61
   Mark 6:6b-13

9. Preach, Teach, And Heal 67
   Mark 6:12-13

10. A Vital Balance 75
    Mark 6:30-34

11. A Problem Of Pollution 81
    Mark 7:1-8, 14-26

12. A Difference Of Opinion 87
    Mark 8:27-38

13. Speculating In Futures 95
    Mark 8:34-35 (27-35)

14. A Man Came Running 101
    Mark 10:17-27

15. Triumphal? Hardly! 109
    Mark 11:1-11

16. Noises In The Vineyard 115
    Mark 12:1-11

17. Sharing The Burden 121
    Mark 12:13-17

18. Who Gives What To The Budget? 127
    Mark 12:41-44

19. The End! 133
    Mark 13:32-37

20. The Divine Drama 141
    Mark 14:12-26

21. The Farewell Meal 147
    Mark 14:12-26

22. Memories And The Sacrament — A Meditation 153
    Mark 14:17-25

23. The Crucifixion 157
    Mark 15:21-32

24. Only The Women Were There 163
    Mark 16:1-8

A Basic Bibliography On The Gospel Of Mark 169

Mark 1:1-11
James 5:7-10
Isaiah 35:1-6, 10

A Wild Man In A Muddy River

Many years ago a number of us were members
    of The Canadian Professors For Peace in the Middle East.
We travelled to Israel with other academics
    from the United States, who were members
        of the American Professors for Peace.
When we visited the Allenby bridge over the Jordan River
    we marveled that anyone would baptize or be baptized
        in such a dirty river.
Surely, it had been much cleaner in the time of
    John The Baptizer and Jesus.
The Feast Day of Saint John The Baptist is June 24th.
It is an exciting day.
This is especially so in the Province of Quebec,
    where John The Baptist is the Patron Saint.
It is a time when fact is just as interesting as fiction.
Every year there is a combination of both.
The late Fr. Irene Beaubien, S.J., used to tell
    an apocryphal story of two French speaking Canadians
        in conversation about the Saint.
One of them is supposed to have said to the other:
    "Where was the Saint born?"
To which his friend replied with authority:
    "In Trois Rivieres."
    "What happened to him?"
    "He was killed by the English when they took Quebec City."
Imagine that you are a business person on an Air Canada flight
    from St. John's, Newfoundland to Toronto, Ontario.
It is a flight that people take every day.

Suppose that just after the plane is airborne a person
    should get up at the front of the business class section
        and begin to make an impassioned address.
He is a fearsome looking character.
Your first terrified reaction is that the aeroplane
    has been taken over by a group of terrorists.
However, his language is fine.
He is fluently bilingual and he carries himself well.
He has a hard, weather-beaten face.
Those near him can detect the scent of an outdoors person.
After the first shock passes of his strange sight and sound,
    his captive audience listens to what he is saying.
Some people recognize that, although he may look quite mad,
    there is truth in his comments.
This is a flight they are not likely ever to forget.
His message is that this plane and others like it
    will reach their destinations in safety.
However, there are people on the plane who will never reach
    the *real* destination of their lives.
He speaks of how good and evil is so mixed up in them
    that one cannot be seen for the other.
He said that big business needs surgery deep and radical,
    if it is to be cured of its obsession with acquiring
        more and more.
There are, he says, companies with harmless titles
    that do big business in selling arms or investing in warfare.
In even the smallest governmental department
    there is naked power bent on self-interest.
The nation which he loves with more passion
    than a Separatist loves Quebec, has become territory
        in the hands of organized crime.
It is a time when any Jezebel can convert a cocktail party
    into a liaison for espionage.
The speaker gives an accurate diagnosis of our sick society.
He is prepared, even compelled,
    to prescribe the cure for the sickness.

His hearers and everyone else must make a spiritual
   "turn around" and start again.
The imaginary man on the plane trip is a parallel
   to a real man who lived on the edge of the wilderness
      many years ago.
He lived in Palestine, not Trois-Rivieres.
The real man, John the Baptist,
   used to meet people on the road
      or by a well in the desert pasture land.
The men he met there were travelling salesmen,
   government civil servants, and desert nomads with their
      sheep.
As they listened to him, a fearsome looking fellow,
   he gave them messages that went straight to the heart of life.
The whole of society, he said, was going mad and getting
   nowhere.
Everywhere some people tried to crush other people
   for a better position, another raise in wages,
      a larger desk, or a better carpet on their office floors.
Had people forgotten that they were created for better things
   than heart attacks and impressive bank accounts?
Or did they believe that God was dead?
   God, said he, is not dead and never has been.
God is alive and about to end the present chaotic society.
The New Kingdom, said John, will emerge after a judgement
   on the way in which both individuals and societies behave.
The business travellers and the nomadic people
   thought about what he had said.
As they watched him, he ate his lunch.
He ate the deluxe lunch on the desert dweller's menu.
   Locusts and wild honey!
      Locusts from bushes, the ground, or the air.
Honey that had been taken from the honeycombs of wild bees,
   whose honeycombs were often in the ground.
His clothing was rough and crude, by contrast
   with the cloaks cut in the Saville Row of Jerusalem.

Before his garments had warmed the back of John,
    they had done the same for some wild beast.
The wilderness,
    really hundreds and hundreds of acres of poor pasture land,
        was the place to which men went to be alone with God.
They went there, not because they were eccentric,
    but because they were sane.
They went there because of a compulsion
    to understand themselves.
A need to receive some insight into *who* they were
    and *why* they had been born.
In the desert John brooded about the state of his country,
    its religious establishment and its government.
All he could see was the judgement of God hanging over it.
What else could people expect who had so deliberately
    flouted both the responsibilities and privileges
        of being the People of God?
            "You are going to be called into question," he said,
            "but you can still do something about it.
            You must do an about-face called repentance.
            And live a life radically different in character
            from the one you are living at the moment."[1]
All sorts of people came to see and hear him.
Some came because their conscience
    would not let them stay away.
Others came because cool reason convinced them
    that something dire was about to happen.
One young man came a distance to hear the wilderness prophet.
Then, he, too, went into the water to be baptized by John.
John said to him:
    "Jesus of Nazareth, what are you doing here?
    I should be coming to you."
Afterward Jesus, like John, went into the desert.
How long was he alone in the desert with his thoughts and God?
We shall never know.
Forty days is simply a symbolic number meaning a long time.
Neither shall we ever know

how deeply Jesus was influenced by John.
Perhaps, as some contend,
   Jesus was, for a time, a disciple of John.
During his ministry, John gathered disciples as Jesus did.
He trained them and sent them out on the trade routes
   to tell other men what he had told them.
His disciples were good men,
   two of whom later became disciples of Jesus.
When John became unpopular with the government of the day
   he was thrown into prison.
He had rebuked Herod Antipas for taking his half-brother's wife.
One evening, in a party mood, Herod told Salome,
   his stepdaughter, to ask for whatever she wanted
      and he would grant it.
Salome checked with Herodias, her mother,
   who was still smouldering about the things John the Baptist
      had said when she married Herod.
That evil woman whispered:
   "Ask him for the head of John the Baptist."
Thus, as Augustine wrote:
   "... an oath that was rashly taken was criminally kept."
His work carried on after his death.
Some thirty years later Paul found about a dozen disciples
   of John in the busy city of Ephesus.
Some of them passed on accounts of their leader,
   just as did the followers of Jesus.
There are many estimates of John and his ministry.
The most interesting for our purpose is the one recorded
by Matthew in which Jesus declared to a crowd:
   "John," he said, "is a brave good man.
   He did not cut his message to suit his hearers.
   If you want to hear only those things that please you,
   then beware of John.
   He bends his message to no one, no matter the pressure."
In a unique word of praise, Jesus said that no one greater
   than John had ever been born.

We can only imagine what that meant to those who heard it!
However, according to Mark, Jesus added a comment
    that seemed to cancel the compliment:
        "But," said Jesus, "even the least in the Kingdom of God
        is greater than John."
By that Jesus issued a challenge to us, not a slight to John.
    "The least in the Kingdom," you and me,
    are not greater than John in what we do or are,
    but in what God does and has done for and through us!
We excel John not in behaviour but in privilege.
John marked the End of an Old Order,
    Jesus was the beginning of the New One.
This did not mean that John should be denied anything
    from the grace of God.
In the scripture there is a parallel between Moses and John.
Moses brought his people to the edge of the Promised Land.
He died before he could enter it.
John brought his people to the edge of the New Age
    and prepared them for the coming of Christ.
He was not himself a member of that Age.
In the plan of God,
    the work of John paved the way for the One who brought
        Good News.
            Hallelujah!
                Amen.

---

1. Frederick C. Grant, *The Gospel According To Mark, Introduction And Exegesis*, The Interpreter's Bible, Vol. VII (New York: Abingdon Press, 1951), p. 657. "As with Jesus, so with John, repentance is 'turning' *from* sin and turning *to* the Lord."

Mark 1:12-13
Romans 5:12-19
Genesis 2:7-9; 3:1-7

Aprons And Fig Leaves

Just for a moment or two,
   I would like you to think about parables.
Imagine you are walking down a busy street in your town.
An acquaintance comes up to you and says:
   "Quickly, name two of Jesus' parables."
After you have got over the surprise of the question,
   and had a good look at the person who asked it,
      what would you say?
Perhaps the Parable of the Good Samaritan?
Maybe also the Parable of the Prodigal Son?
Both parables come from Luke, the Master Story Teller.
They are amongst the most familiar parables of Jesus.
In the hands of Jesus, the use of a parable,
   as an aid to communicating an important message,
      had reached its peak.
His people loved parables.[1]
They had been telling parables for years.
   Hundreds of years.
   Thousands of years before Jesus.
Sometimes they told parables as an answer
   to the basic questions that come up in every generation.
      Was the world always as it is now?
      No? Well, then, by whom was it created?
      How was it done?
      Were people like you and me created at the same time
      as the lion and the chickadee and the worm?
      Why is there evil in the world?
      Does God *allow* it? Or does it *allow* God?

These are religious questions.
The great religious questions, such as these,
    are not answered in the way we answer technical questions.
The great religious questions
    are not answered in a scientific textbook, certainly!
Answers there will be changed with every new edition.
Religious questions are answered in a religious way.[2]
    Most often they are answered through parables.
        Parables are told in the language of beautiful poetry.
Parables such as are recorded
    in the first eleven chapters of Genesis.
We read parts of two of them this morning.
In his day Jesus heard those same parables read in the synagogue.
Doesn't that send a thrill down your spine?
It does mine!
You and I and Jesus have in common this much at least,
    that all of us have listened to the same parables.
He heard it in one language. We in another.
He heard it 2,000 years ago. We did this morning.
The parable has to do with the matter of temptation.
Our spiritual ancestors, the Hebrew people, knew
    that everyone experienced temptation.
        All the time.
Teenagers like Rachel and David,
    their grandparents Isaac and Sarah,
        all alike experienced temptation.
How they were tempted depended mainly on their ages,
    on their natures and on their particular personal situations.
Without exception, all of them were tempted.
The temptations changed, of course, over time.
Many of the things that tempted teenagers then,
    and that tempt teenagers now, changed over time.
Many of the things that tempt a present day teenager,
    have no temptation at all for their parents or grandparents.
That doesn't mean we are unable to remember
    what some of them were like.

Modern teenagers are confronted with temptations
    about which the rest of us know nothing at all.
Where and when did it all begin?
    This matter of temptation.
Is it so much a part of our nature
    that we are unable ever to escape it?
Were we always subject to temptation?
The answer to these questions is the purpose of the parable.
One of our spiritual ancestors,
    with profound insights into human nature,
        replied in a parable as unforgettable as any told by Jesus.
Once upon a time, it began, when the world was young,
    our ancestors shared a common experience.
It was such a basic experience that it had to do with God,
    and their relationship with God.
Right from the beginning, the relationship
    between God and our ancestors was a unique one.
It was a relationship totally unlike the relationship
    between the Creator and trees, and turtles, and tigers.
These cannot be, and are not ever tempted as we are.
They cannot and do not rebel against their Creator.
They begin life, they grow old and they die.
    They fulfill the purpose of their creation.
        They never want the place of God in creation!
Only persons are tempted as we know temptation.
    Temptation is our human problem.
It always had been — right from the beginning.
We want the place that belongs to God in our lives.
    We want to be the centre of our universe.
Little children play a harmless game
    and sing a child's lines:
        "I am the king of the castle
        and you are a dirty rascal."
It is a child's game.
Yet, it reflects the human temptation
    to be the centre of our universe.
        What I want is all that is important to me!

Last winter, in a career counselling situation
    in one of the city high schools, a young person said:
        "This is my life, and no one, but no one
        is going to tell me how to live it."
Similarly, in the face of a request for human compassion
    or consideration, comes a selfish adult response:
        "What's in it for me?"
In the sort of society in which we live today,
    the attitude is increasingly:
        you must look out for number one.
When we think and speak like that we are making it plain
    that we are the centre of our lives.
    "This is my life and I intend to live it my way.
    I am going to get out of it whatever I can.
    I will play the part of God in my life.
    I will decide what is right or wrong for me.
        MOVE OVER, GOD!"
However, according to the Bible,
    there is something seriously wrong here.
We were not created to think primarily about ourselves.
We were created to love and serve God,
    and to love and serve the people of God.
All of them. Of whatever colour, race, or religion.
Otherwise we are going through life
    with a distorted view of ourselves in the scheme of things.
One day, many years ago, as little children
    we were taken to an amusement centre.
We were taken through the house of mirrors.
It was a scary experience for a little child.
Although the tour did not last long,
    some children cried to be taken out of it.
They were afraid of what they saw in the mirrors.
In one mirror you were four feet tall and four feet wide.
In another you were all head, mostly nose.
In another eight feet tall and eight inches wide.
The point is that the image, the picture,
    of who we were was distorted in the mirrors.

That, according to both Testaments,
    is precisely the human situation.
With ourselves as the centre of the world,
    we are not as we were intended by God to be.
The temptation to be God, to make our own decisions
    about things right or wrong, distorts our image.
We become something or someone other
    than we were intended to be.
When we are exposed for what we are,
    we will always makes excuses.
Excuses to cover our selfishness.
    Excuses to cover our wobbly morals.
        Excuses to cover our pretence
            that we were doing the will of God.
Which just happened to be the same as our own will.
This is especially true for religious people.
The Parable of The Fall teaches us that temptation
    was there right from the beginning.
It is a human experience, as human as the experiences
    of hunger or anger or sex or curiosity.
It was a test our ancestors flunked!
That failure was understood as a mirror of all humanity.
It was just the way we were and always would be.
Then, we come to the story of the temptations of Jesus.
Jesus must have told the experience himself.
There was no one else in the desert with him.
In the Gospel of Matthew,
    the writer tells of three temptations.
Mark writes simply that:
    "He was in the wilderness forty days, tempted by Satan ...
    and was with the wild beasts, and the angels ministered unto
    him."
Jesus endured real temptations!
The nearer one's relationship with God,
    the greater the temptation to have the place of God.
The nearer one's relationship with God,
    the more serious the temptation to defect from the will of God.

If that is not so, then every saint is a liar!
The writer of another New Testament book says of Jesus:
> "... he was in all points tempted in the same ways we are, and he resisted all of them."

Ah, now *that* is Good News!
When I am tempted to make a funny story more amusing
than it was then I know that he was, too.
When you are tempted to be selfish or jealous or proud,
remember that once upon a time he was tempted
in precisely the same way.
When I am tempted to exercise power over another human being,
in any way at all, then I remember that he was, as well.
When you are tempted to pay no attention whatever to a sermon,
then know that he was tempted likewise in the Synagogue.
That is Good News!
It is human to experience temptation.
We share that with Jesus.
We may share with Jesus as well
something of the power he had to resist temptation.
When Jesus told the disciples of his experiences with temptation,
he was telling them of his own experiences as well.
Except that he had overcome them.
He had resisted every attempt to give in to temptation.
When he told Jesus' story of victory in the desert,
Mark used a word that can only mean that his temptations
would go on until the end of his life!
So they did.
We know that from his prayer in the Garden of Gethsemane.
The power of temptation was always whispering in his ear.
The snake with the apple in its mouth was always
within sight or sound until the crucifixion itself.
Temptation is *never* over and done with.
We meet each temptation as if it were the first
and worst we have ever encountered.
As Christian people we meet it with the example of Jesus,
knowing that it may be defeated.

As Christian people, we meet temptation relying
   on our obedience to God in order to defeat it.
We meet each temptation with the possibility of victory.
Because at some time in our lives
   we made a commitment to God as the centre of life.
A commitment we renew as often as we possibly can.
Then, although nothing is ever guaranteed,
   there is no necessity at least,
      to reach for the fig leaves in order to make an apron.
      Hallelujah!
         Amen.

---

1. We need only think of the parables throughout the Old Testament, beginning with Genesis.

    Harvey K. McArthur & Robert W. Johnston, *They Also Taught In Parables*. Rabbinic Parables From the First Centuries of the Christian Era (Grand Rapids, Michigan: Academie Books, 1990).

    Joachim Jeremias, *Rediscovering The Parables* (London: S.C.M. Press, Billings and Sons, Ltd., 1966), pp. 22ff.

2. W.R. Telford, *The Theology Of The Gospel Of Mark* (Cambridge, U.K.: Cambridge University Press, 2003), pp. 21, 102, 129.

Mark 2:1-12
Corinthians 1:18-22
Isaiah 43:18-35

A Visible Sign

The word "sin" had been used three times in ten minutes.
That was strange, because people who used it
    were not in Church at the time.
They were together in the waiting area
    of an out-patient department.
A mother was explaining to a friend
    how it was her son had caught pneumonia.
    "Jason went out that warm day without his jacket," she said.
    "He played street hockey all evening and got a bad chill.
    He was so sick I thought he was likely to die."
Her friend replied:
    "What a sin, my dear, what a sin."
A few minutes later
    a heavy policeman walked through the waiting area.
He was escorting a person who looked rather the worse for wear.
The person was recognized at once by several people.
After he disappeared down the corridor,
    one lady said to her neighbour:
    "It's a sin to waste the health service on the likes of that!
    He's no sooner set straight than he is back at it again."
Later, in her consulting room,
    one of the doctors used the word "sin" again.
She was thinking in particular about certain diseases
    transmitted through sexual contact.
She said to her patient:
    "What does the Church have to say these days
    about the relationship between sin and disease?
    Or does it have anything to say at all?"

If these three conversations
>were all you had to go on, you might conclude
>>that we live in a society especially conscious of sin!

The Gospel lesson this morning
>assumes that sin and sickness belong together.

It takes for granted
>that forgiveness and healing belong together as well.

The question then is:
>"Who may forgive sins so that healing may take place?"

The relationship between sin and disease
>is an old and complicated one.

Certainly there are many serious illnesses
>that have nothing whatever to do with personal wrongdoing.

There are other illnesses
>that have more to do with carelessness
>>or a deliberate mistreatment of our bodies
>>>than they have to do with "sin" of any kind.

The boy who caught pneumonia playing street hockey
>was careless of his body — as boys are apt to be.

The man who drank to excess was guilty of mistreating his body.
>As some people are.

However, the scriptures are concerned
>with more than carelessness or mistreatment,
>>however sinful these things may be.

In the literature of our spiritual ancestors
>the connection between healing and forgiveness
>>was a close one.

One of the rabbis had written:
>"The sick man will not get up from his bed
>until all his sins are forgiven."[1]

The Gospel of Mark was written by a person who agreed with that.

He told six stories to illustrate the authority of Jesus
>to forgive sins so that healing might take place.

We read one of these stories this morning.

It is about a man who is paralyzed.

Although the paralysis wasn't bad at first,

if got a little worse every day.
Eventually he was unable to move.
   He had to be moved by other people.
The family tried everything for him.
   It had all come to nothing.
Then, one hot morning, four of his old friends
   were speaking together about him.
These friends were imaginative people.
   We know that.
Less imaginative people shrug their shoulders
   and accept a situation as it is.
Less imaginative people
   avoid doing anything new or different.
They pretend that the daily routine is more important.
   "Has the mail come yet?"
   "When will dinner be ready?"
Other men and women are decisive
   and impulsive by nature.
They do things, as well as talk
   about what might or ought to be done.
   "Let's try the young Rabbi from Nazareth,"
   said one of them.
So, they made a stretcher.
They put their friend's thin mat or rug on it.
They moved him over onto it, and away they went.
When they arrived at the house where Jesus was speaking
   they couldn't get near it!
      It was blocked out.
         The situation looked hopeless.
In exasperation they went up onto the roof.
The roof was a flat surface.
It was made of earth
   over a framework of closely woven sticks.[2]
It had been packed hard.
The earth was five to seven inches deep!
The young men began to open it up.

Within minutes there was chaos in the room below.
The dirt and dust of the earthen roof began to fall
> on the crowd that had gathered to hear Jesus.

Dust and dirt got into their eyes,
> so that they couldn't see.

It got into their noses.
> They began to cough and sneeze.

The noise of the falling earth and breaking wood
> drowned out the words of Jesus below.

Within minutes the crowd was angry.
The man of the house was beside himself.
> "Get down off the roof!
> Who are you anyway? What do you want?"

There was no answer.
> The hole just got bigger.

Suddenly, the large hole in the roof was darkened over.
Down through the hole came a stretcher.
On the stretcher lay a frightened, paralyzed man.
Little wonder if he was frightened.
> He had never been airborne before!

This wasn't the first time people had come to Jesus
> in desperate circumstances.

A blind man had called to him from the side of the road,
> even though people had tried to keep him quiet.

A woman crept through the crowd to touch his robe,
> never thinking he would notice she had done it.

A messenger brought him to the bedroom of a dying servant,
> and so on it went.

This case was different.
The men who brought the paralytic were risking arrest
> for breaking, entering, and malicious damage.

In Jesus' day these were serious crimes,
> involving long terms in prison and sometimes worse.

These men were desperate.
They were *determined*
> to bring their friend to Jesus of Nazareth.

Jesus interpreted their desperation and determination
    as faith in God.
So, he said to the paralyzed person,
    "My son, your sins are forgiven you."[3]
What's *this*?
The man was paralyzed wasn't he?
The text doesn't say he was the
    greatest sinner in Capernaum!
What then had sin and forgiveness to do
    with his healing and wholeness?
The religious people didn't like what they had seen and heard.
There were people who dealt with disease.
They were called Healers
Only God dealt with "sin."
In this story, as Mark tells it, the young teacher
from Nazareth claimed the right
    and authority to do both.
In the person of Jesus
    the one activity involved the other one as well.
    "Rise, take up your bed and walk."
That would have been the more acceptable thing to say.
That would have dealt with the immediate problem.
No one would have argued with that.
What if the immediate problem was merely a symptom,
    of what was really wrong with the man?
Anyone with average eyesight
    is able to see the physical expression of paralysis.
Surely it makes more sense to say:
    "Rise, you may go home now,"
than it is to say:
    "Your sins are forgiven you."
In this case, according to Mark,
    the first command would deal with the symptom.
The second would deal with the root cause
    of a paralyzed life.
Pills, surgery, and therapy deal effectively

with the causes and symptoms
of many serious problems.
In some cases, though, according to Jesus,
real healing may have to wait for treatment
on a different, deeper, level entirely.
It is a wonderful story, isn't it?
It was a great favourite in the Early Church.
It deals primarily with the *authority* of Jesus
and with the *mission* of the Church.[4]
It deals with the authority of Jesus
to forgive the sins we commit against God,
and against one another.
In this story, the One who has the authority,
in the Name of God, to heal the diseases of the body,
is also able to deal with the troubles of the soul.
These are the most serious troubles of all.
The Church traces back to Jesus,
and to this story of the paralytic and his healing,
the pattern for its mission in the world.
That mission has to do with the *forgiveness* of sins,
however we may express it.
And with the *healing* of lives paralyzed in many different ways.
Sometimes the paralysis comes as much
from our treatment at the hands of other people,
as it does from what we have done ourselves.
In the midst of an increasingly secular society
there is a visible sign of that forgiveness and healing.
That sign is the Church of Jesus Christ.
The Church has within its life
the priceless treasure of pardon and healing.
It is a treasure given the Church by her Lord himself.
The Church of Jesus Christ,
in any place where the Gospel is preached,
has become the sign of healing and pardon!
The community of believers,
of which this congregation is one,
is the custodian of healing, wholeness, and pardon.

The *mission* of the Church to offer forgiveness
is also its responsibility to *provide it*,
to every paralyzed person with whom it comes in contact.
Amen.

---

1. Nedarim, 41a.

2. C.E.B. Cranfield, *The Gospel According To St. Mark* (Cambridge University Press: Cambridge, 2000), p. 97. Originally printed in 1959. Reprinted many times.

3. John R. Donahue, S.J., and Daniel J. Harrington, S.J., *The Gospel of Mark* (The Liturgical Press: Collegeville, Minnesota, 2002), pp. 94ff.

4. Norman Perrin and Dennis C. Duling, *The New Testament: An Introduction* (Harcourt Brace Javanovich, Inc: New York, 1982), p. 244. "These stories have a definite function: to exhibit the authority of Jesus in deeds, just as his teaching and his calling of disciples exhibit it in words."

Mark 3:13-15, 19b-30
2 Corinthians 4:13—5:1
Genesis 3:9-15

Lord Of The Flies

The title of this sermon has nothing to do
    with a novel of the same name, by William Golding.
It has, rather, to do with Jesus
    and those who heard him teaching.
The novel has partly to do with those who are within
    and those who are without the establishment.
What is meant by the word "establishment"?
Do you consider yourself a member of it?
It is one of those labels we use
    that no one takes time to define.
We use it to describe other people and their institutions,
    often in an uncomplimentary manner.
The family unit may or may not be a part of the establishment.
It *is* if it teaches respect for the body, mind, and spirit
    of each member within it.
It *is* not if the father or mother is adulterous,
    the teenagers are promiscuous, and if everyone
        in the family unit uses certain four letter words.
The family unit is then termed "progressive,"
    rather than "establishment."
The school system is considered a part of the establishment,
    if it supports the learning process in an acceptable manner.
It *is* if it is concerned with the development of the whole person
    and his or her relationship to the community.
If, on the other hand, learning is secondary and all forms
    of self-expression are primary matters,
        the school is not a part of the establishment.
The Church is understood to be a part of the establishment.

It *is* if it teaches its members how to pray
  with and for one another.
It *is* if it provides opportunities for worship in public.
It *is* if it is concerned with you and your relationship with God.
It *is* if it enlists and develops people
  as disciples of Jesus Christ.
If, on the other hand, the Church is more concerned
  with our social adjustments and our place in society,
    it is irrelevant and not "establishment."
It is irresponsible to label anyone a member of the establishment
  because the word means something different to each one of us.
All that is best in society is in some sense a part of the
  "establishment," just as all that is worst in society
    is a part of the established order as well.
You might also say the same sort of thing for other labels.
When I asked whether you consider yourself a member
of the establishment, all I wanted was to get you
thinking about some of the labels we put on one another.
And why we do so.
The label given you by other people is intended, in some sense,
  as a description of you or of your group.
It may be accurate or complimentary, or it may not.
It simply means that there are people to whom you represent
  an influence of some sort in your community.
When people were confronted with Jesus of Nazareth,
  as he shared with them his radical views of God and people,
    they put labels on him.
The Gospels tell us about some of these labels.
At one time his mother, brothers, and sisters
  thought he needed psychiatric attention.
He is "beside himself," they said.
They meant that he had worked himself into a state
  of mental excitement.
They took his strange words and actions as the expression
  of a person who had become a religious fanatic.
In other words, he was, they thought, in the grip
  of an awesome and evil power!

There were other people to whom Jesus was a source
   of freedom and of "new life."
These were people who saw God set free from the restrictions
   and regulations in which their religion had bound God.
They recognized his healing and preaching power
   as coming from God.
They, too, wanted to share in this divine power.
Partly out of curiosity, partly out of conviction,
   there were other devout people who wondered whether
      Jesus was not the person for whom their nation
         had been waiting — for centuries.
They remembered the old titles and asked one another:
   "Do you think he could be the promised Son of David?"
   "How do we know this man is not the Christ, the Messiah?"
To all of which the religious and political authorities replied:
   "This man is Be'elzebub himself,
   the 'Lord of the Flies.' "
Or, is it by the authority of the Lord of the Flies
   that he performs his demonstrations of power?
The Lord of the Flies was thought to be one of the most
   powerful of the forces of evil in the ancient world.
"The Lord of the Flies" was a title given to the devil
   when it was at its worst abroad in the world.
The fact that people used strong language
   when speaking about Jesus is itself an indication
      that there was something quite extraordinary about him.
Those whose influence for good or evil is never felt
   are not given labels, either of admiration or contempt.
The extraordinary influence of Jesus on his followers
   and hearers attracted attention and demanded a response
      from them.
Jesus was sensitive to the labels he was given,
   because they were vital to the mission given him by God.
"The Lord of the Flies" was not the first label he rejected.
He rejected it as much for his followers as for himself.
He played on the use of this label to create a contrast

between his work and the forces of evil.
He used the label to point out the nature of his work
and how it was consistent with the will of God.
He agreed with his opponents that a person might be
an instrument either of good or evil.
The function of the destructive powers,
the powers of evil, is to produce madness,
to incite violence, to cause pain and disease,
and to promote lies.
"Is it not unusual," he asked, "that I should be healing
diseased bodies, relieving pain, and ridding people
of the evil powers that create madness and that incite
violence?"
As well as defeating lies with the truth.
Would I be doing these things
if I were the Lord of the Flies, if I were in partnership
with Satan?
The devil would not keep someone in his service
who had undone all the things he had managed to arrange.
Secondly, this title, according to Jesus,
included the only sin that is without forgiveness.
Those who were guilty of the unforgivable sin on this occasion
had witnessed something that could have come only from God.
Rather than recognize it as such,
they identified the good things of God as evil.
They were blinded by their personal prejudices and antagonisms
and as a result they were unable to see the power of God
at work through Jesus amongst the People of God.
"As long as people insist on not knowing the difference between
good and evil, right and wrong, it is not possible for them to
come into touch ..." with the power of God.
The final rejection of God is to identify good as evil.
This is the only unpardonable sin.[1]
This is the sin against the Spirit of God.
It is a sin of which we are in danger simply by refusing
to accept as good that which the Spirit of Christ

>   does in the world.
> Possibly in ways that are not familiar to us
>   or that we did not expect.
> What is there in a name or a label?
> There is a great deal.
> A name may be affectionate or hostile,
>   destructive or protective.
> Whatever the case, a label or name, when applied to Jesus,
>   is an important symbol of belief.
> There is much to be learned from the names or labels
>   by which Jesus was and is called.
> To some a fanatic, to others a madman,
>   to many others the Saviour of body, mind, and soul.
> Once upon a time he was called The Lord of the Flies
>   by those to whom he came as the messenger of God.
> As Christians we have names, labels, for Jesus
>   found on the lips of no one else:
>   to us he is supremely the Man of Love, the Lord of Life,
>   the Great Physician of body, mind, and spirit!
>   Amen.

---

1. Lamar Williamson, Jr., *Mark* (Atlanta: John Knox Press, 1983), pp. 80ff.

Mark 3:19b-30
2 Kings 1:2-18

Mistaken Identity!

There is a businessperson in Chilliwack
   who is frequently mistaken for someone else.
He is mistaken for a certain provincial politician.
   The politician belongs to a different party
      and this person is, therefore, not impressed.
         He is annoyed.
Have you ever been mistaken for someone else?
Who was it?
When you are mistaken for someone else
   it is not always amusing or to your advantage.
One morning I was at a local Tim Horton's.
Through the window as I was going into the building,
   I could see a man staring at me.
Because I was alone, I sat by the window
   at a small table for two people.
The other man was seated four tables away from me.
   At this point, he was simply glaring at me.
He was quite clearly angry about something.
I thought of all the people I might have annoyed recently.
   He was not one of them.,
Eventually, he shouted: "Hey, you!"
   Now, normally, I don't answer to "Hey, you."
This time I did. "Yes?"
He said: "You are the used car salesman, right?"
"No," I said, "I am not a used car salesman."
By this time there was not another conversation in the room.
Everyone was listening to him.
   "Oh yes, you are," he said. "I know you.
   You sold me that so-and-so Ford out there."

"I wouldn't sell anyone a Ford," I said,
"I certainly wouldn't sell one to you."
"I intend to get my money back," he said. "All of it."
"I hope you do," I replied, "If you are so unhappy with your car. Good Luck."
With that, he was so angry
he got up from his table and came over to mine.
He looked down at me and said:
"You are a used car salesman, aren't you?"
"No, I am not."
"Well, who are you then? What do you do?"
"I am a minister. The scattered time I preach the Gospel."
"O my God," he replied.
"Exactly," was all I could think of saying.
"May I sit down?" he asked. "I would like to tell you my story."
He told me his story.
It was one of the worst stories I had ever heard.
It was easy, then, to understand why the poor fellow
might want to find someone to blame for his hard life.
It was a case of mistaken identity.
Some of us are never mistaken for anyone really important.
For example, I am never mistaken
for Wayne Gretzky or Billy Graham or Pope Benedict the XVI!
That is strange.
There must surely be a resemblance of some kind
to one or other of them.
However, I was once mistaken for an important person.
It was in 1995, in Victoria.
Three of us had gone to the beautiful Buchart Gardens.
At one point we decided to go our separate ways.
Two went off to see some special roses.
I went off to sit in the quiet by a duck pond.
Suddenly, an American tourist came up to me and,
peering through very thick glasses, said:

"Excuse me, Sir, you are Mr. Gorbachev,
the former Premier of Russia, aren't you?"
"No, Madam, I am not former Premier Gorbachev."
She went on to peer and said:
"I am sorry, Sir, but I would know you anywhere.
I promise not to tell anyone you are here.
May I ask you, please, to sit over there by the gazebo?
I would love to have a photograph to show the folks back home.
My home is in Mobile, Alabama, and this would blow them away."
After a few minutes, there was no point protesting any more.
So, I replied:
"Certainly, Madam, but let's do this quickly.
Other people might recognize me as well."
Then, after some fussing about,
she took my picture to prove to the folks back home,
that she had met Premier Gorbachev in Victoria.
Then the same lady asked me to sign a postcard.
"My husband Victor wouldn't come on this holiday," she said.
"I would just love to have a souvenir for him."
So, I signed it:
"With best wishes for Victor, from Michael Gorbachev."
It was a case of mistaken identity.
Helped on a lot by her bad eyesight.
As you know from the New Testament,
Jesus was often mistaken for someone else.
Sometimes it was simply a well meaning mistake.
A complimentary mistake.
For example, because he was such a superb Teacher,
there were people, lots of them,
who thought he might be Moses come back from the dead.
That was the highest compliment Jesus could be paid.
In Jesus' day, his people believed that Moses
was the greatest person who ever lived up to that time.

The people governed every aspect of their lives
   by what they believed Moses had taught them.
He was the greatest of all the prophets.
   Prophets were people who spoke for God.
Then, too, Jesus was sometimes mistaken for Elijah.
   Jesus' people were waiting for Elijah to return to his people.
The coming of Elijah would announce
   the beginning of the End of the world.
To be mistaken for Elijah,
   an outstanding person to the people,
      was almost as important as being mistaken for Moses.
        It was a great compliment!
After the tyrannical King Herod had beheaded John the Baptist
   there were people, even Herod himself,
      who thought John had come back to life as Jesus.
All these were cases of mistaken identity.
They were all attempts to answer the question:
   "Who is Jesus?"
Unhappily, Jesus was not always mistaken for someone great.
   For someone who spoke and acted on behalf of God.
There were people who claimed Jesus was someone evil.
We know that from the New Testament.
One time he was called "Be'elzebub,"
   a name that means "The Lord Of The Flies."
It was the same as saying:
   "You are the king of the devils."
On another occasion he was told:
   "You *have* a devil!" or,
   "You are possessed by the devil!"
Maybe it would be the same thing as saying to Jesus:
   "You are the Big Boss of the Hell's Angels."
The oldest sin of all is to call someone EVIL, when that someone
   is good.
It is also one of the most modern sins.
According to the New Testament
   it is the sin against the Holy Spirit.

It is the *only* unforgivable sin.
In Jesus day it was done by people pretending
    to be concerned for matters moral and religious.
It was a slander shouted in the marketplace.
    Or gossiped in the streets.
        Or whispered in the Temple.
It was demonic, devilish then, and it still is.
In our day it is done by people
    with much less courage, still pretending to be concerned
        for matters moral and religious.
Today it may be done on television, over the telephone,
    the internet, the radio, or in the newspaper.
        It may come from a poison pen, in an unsigned letter.
Who is Jesus?
That is the question that lies behind the Gospel story.
What does it mean to call Jesus the Messiah? The Christ?
That is the question the Church has tried to answer,
    right from the beginning.
As Christian people
    we believe that Jesus is both like God and like us.
What we know about God, what we believe about God,
    we know and believe from the words and actions of Jesus.
It is always easier for us to believe
    that Jesus is like God,
        than it is to believe that Jesus is like us!
To some extent
    we believe that Jesus is more like God than he is like us,
        to protect ourselves.
The more we claim that Jesus is like God,
    the less he has to do with you and me.
After all,
    how could we be expected to behave like God?
        Or to imitate God?
If we cannot be like God, and we cannot,
    then we can excuse our greed,
        our lack of love, our lack of compassion,

> our intolerance of people unlike us,
> our failures to forgive.

Why?
> Because we are *only* human!

Only God is able to rise above our human weaknesses.
When we admit that Jesus is also like us, and he is,
> then everything in life is challenged and changed.

The more we admit that Jesus is like us,
> the more we need every excuse in the Book
> > to cover our words and actions,
> > > — when they are unlike those of Jesus.

Who is Jesus?
> He is the One who lived and died for other people.
> > He is the One who lived and died for you and for me.

He is the One who lives today and forever
> within the People of God.

Jesus is the One by whom our lives are being transformed,
> however slowly or suddenly.

Or sadly, in some people, not at all.
Who is Jesus?
> He is your Lord and mine!

Any other answer is simply a case of mistaken identity!
> > Amen.

Mark 3:26-35
2 Corinthians 5:6-10
Ezekiel 17:22-24

You Are Family!

There are few families in which misunderstandings do not occur.
A husband may be misunderstood by his wife.
    Or the wife by her husband.
Children may be misunderstood by their parents
    and parents by their children.
In this respect, according to the Gospel of Mark,
    the family of Jesus was no exception.
As a young man, Jesus was misunderstood,
    particularly by his mother.
When he left home to travel about the country
    the other young men of his age in the village were already
        married and settled down.
The word of him that came back to Nazareth linked him
    with one of the groups of men who were wandering
        from city to city.
His old friends at home were confused and concerned
    over the strange behaviour of Joseph's son.
Some people suggested he might have become mentally unwell.
There were others, less charitable by far,
    who saw in him the devil at work.
Her worry about him got the better of his mother.
She went in search of her eldest son,
    taking with her those of his brothers and sisters
        who were still living at home.
They found him, surrounded by people.
Finding it impossible to catch his attention,
    she sent him a message that she was there.
A person nearest to Jesus passed it on to him.

"Your mother and sisters and brothers are here.
They want to speak with you."
Jesus used the unexpected arrival of his family to illustrate
what he had been teaching.
He used his family as the basis for what he wanted to teach
about the family of faith.
The human family is made up of people
who share a particular blood relationship.
In it there are loyalties based on common parentage.
Within it there are restrictions and freedoms based
on mutual respect for the human dignity of parent and child.
As well as for the welfare of society.
In the family of faith there are people
whose life together issues from a common loyalty to God.
In the family of faith there are people created
in the image and likeness of God.
Just as in a human family there are people created
in the image and likeness of mother and father.
Or of grandmother and grandfather.
The family of faith, by whatever name it is known,
in common with the family of John Smith,
derives its strength through placing its first loyalty
beyond the ties of common race or even of common
creed.
Jesus taught that when we take seriously the place of God
in human life, we will take seriously the rights and claims
of those with whom we live and work and worship.
"Whoever does the will of God is my mother,
my brother, and my sister."
As one biblical scholar has written of these verses:
"Alienated from his natural family, Jesus has created
a new family that consists of those whom he has called
to follow him. Alienated from the Jewish leadership,
he can be found to redefine custom, tradition, or even law,
to recline at table with tax collectors and sinners and have
dealings with Gentiles or outcasts."[1]

It was a story of Jesus, misunderstood by his human family.
Christian people believe that the worth and dignity of human affection is valued most by those who recognize the supremacy of God in their lives.
We shall have something worthwhile to offer one another when we have first given our lives to the will of God as we understand it in the person of Jesus Christ.
This places family relationships on a high level.
It also underlines what ought to be the relationship
    to one who belongs to the same family of faith.
Perhaps it was precisely because Jesus had known the meaning
    of family life and love that he could use it to illustrate the
        nature of the community of faith.
    "My mother, my brothers, and my sisters
    are those who do the will of God."
Doubtless, his family in Nazareth was precious to him.
He could use its early intimacies as a reflection
    of the relationship that ought to exist between those
        who belong to the family of God.
Normally, members of the same family make allowances
    for one another, despite jealousies, greed, even betrayals.
In an old issue of the *Scots* magazine was a true story
    by a then-elderly father.
The story described a long ago experience with his widowed father.
His father was a successful sheep farmer.
He had spent a lifetime improving his flock
    and the land on which it grazed.
An only son had been with the father all his life
    and both of them took for granted that one day
        the son would take over where his father had left off.
As time went by the son began to have second thoughts
    about his future.
The more he thought about it the more he knew
    he did not want to be a sheep farmer.
He wanted instead to study law and become a lawyer.
The issue was brought to a head one day when his father

said to him:
> "Tonight we must have a talk about this farm.
> I want to give it to you now, so that I may enjoy
> seeing you have the good of it."

All that long day the son wondered how he would tell his father
of his change in plans.

When the evening came and the lamp was lit,
the father gave a cough to indicate that the important
matter was about to be discussed.

Before he could say a word, the son blurted out:
> "Father, I don't want to be a sheep farmer. I want to be a
> lawyer instead. I will be leaving for Glasgow in the morning
> to see about it."

There followed a shocked silence.
Neither man spoke to one another.

After a time the father went upstairs to bed.

The son spent a sleepless night, wondering whether
he had broken his father's heart.

In the morning they had breakfast together,
almost as if nothing had happened between them.

In a pause, the father asked his son:
> "Thomas, how much money will you need?"

Fifty years later, the son said this was the most
magnificent thing anyone had ever said to him!

Even when his father had been terribly disappointed,
he gave his son what encouragement he needed.

Even when he did not understand the reason
for his son's decision, he gave him his support.

They belonged to one another in such a deep way
that nothing like the matter of the night before
could separate the father from the son he loved.
Or the son from his father.

Mary may not have understood the meaning of her son's life.
She did understand that when he was dying she should be there.
The brothers of Jesus may not have understood why
he had left his family and home to wander about the

country with a group of other young men.
Yet, after the resurrection some of them were active
   in the early church.
They risked their lives just as he had risked his.
In this passage from Mark's gospel, when he used his family
   as an illustration, Jesus stretched wide the boundaries
      of the family of the People of God.
   "My brothers, sisters, and mother," he said, "are not only
   those with whom I was brought up in Nazareth;
   they are not limited even to my best friends
   and neighbours. Nor to those who
   worship God in the same place and way I do."
In the National Gallery there hung for many years a painting
   regarded as an outstanding work on the Holy Family.
In the lower third of the canvas
   was an artistic impression of Joseph, Mary, and Jesus.
It was taken down some twenty years ago for a thorough cleaning.
The cleaning process revealed that the upper part of the canvas
   had at some time been painted over.
The upper part had been hidden from view.
When the painting was restored the upper part was seen
   as the completion of the lower.
In it was a figure to represent God, as Father,
   and another figure for God, as Holy Sprit.
The artist has so skilfully painted the upper
   and lower portions of the canvas that Jesus was seen to be
      the third member, the one in common to each group.
The restoration brought to light the symbolism
   common to both the human family and to the family of faith.
As his disciples, at the centre of each and common
   to both is the faith we have in God through Jesus Christ.
The family of faith is as wide as the range of those
   who both know and do the will of God.
It will increase in number and variety
   until it has within it all those for whom our Lord
      put obedience to God above all else.

Even above human family affection.
Doing the will of God above all else in the world.
                Amen.

---

1. Jack Dean Kingsbury, *The Christology of Mark* (Philadelphia: Fortress Press, 1989), p. 52.

Mark 4:1-9
Matthew 13:1-9
Luke 8:4-8

A Model For Mission

This is a story about George Munro.
He had applied for a position with a supermarket chain.
After he was hired, he was selected for a course on salesmanship.
George likes people and he found the course interesting and easy.
He passed it without a problem,
    with grades well above the average.
Before he could begin selling his products
    he had one more test to pass.
The sales supervisor gave him a list of stores
    and a list of store managers to visit for possible sales.
Unknown to George,
    he was being observed by an experienced salesperson
        as he entered and left each one of the stores.
Also unknown to George,
    each manager had been asked not to buy anything from him.
        In some cases to be rude and difficult as well.
He was being tested to see how well
    he could handle rejection and disappointment.
He walked into the first store
    with a confident step and with his head held high.
His visit was unsuccessful.
He came out of the store showing a little disappointment.
He went from one store to the other,
    with less confidence each time,
        but still trying to put up a good front.
As the morning wore on
    he became more and more disappointed and discouraged.
It showed in the way he walked.

    In the way he talked.
        How he thought about himself.
Finally, at 11:30 he decided *not* to try again.
Instead, he went to Tim Horton's for a coffee.
    The company decided not to hire him.
They felt he was unable to deal with failure.
    He couldn't handle rejection.
Now, part of the problem belonged with George.
    He had expected only a successful visit to each store.
Part of the problem was in the training he had been given.
    He had not been prepared for rejection.
It was something like that with the disciples
    when Jesus began to preach and teach.
He and his disciples,
    were working in a district they knew well.
They met with two very different responses.
In the first instance,
    there was serious hostility from religious leaders.
Jesus and his followers
    seemed to break all the religious rules, deliberately.
    "Look at the company he keeps," said his critics, "and did you hear where they *were* last week?"
    "We know the sort of people who go there, don't we?"
    "Did you hear what they *did* last week?"
    "And, they went for a walk on our Holy Day."
    "He cured a sick person on our Holy Day."
Eventually, the opposition was so hostile to Jesus
    that he had to leave the towns for the country.
That was one result of the campaign.
The other side of the campaign in Galilee
    was the apparent enthusiasm of ordinary people.
On one occasion the crowds were so huge
    that Jesus had to use a floating pulpit.
He sat in a boat just off shore
    and preached to the crowds from there.
Yet, he knew and the disciples knew

       that despite the crowds *listening* to him
          it didn't mean that anyone *heard* what he was saying.
The main question on the minds of the disciples was:
    "Why does so much effort produce so little result?"
       The disciples were "down."
          They were ready to give up.
So he told them a parable, a story, to illustrate
    what was happening in the Galilean campaign.
The Early Church passed on the story
    to illustrate what has happened in every campaign
        for the Gospel since then.
The parable also illustrates what happens
    in the personal experience of every Christian person
        at some time or other in his or her life.
The parable is of a farmer sowing grain.
Even before he did the sowing
    the farmer knew that some seed would be wasted.[1]
        He knew that not every seed would germinate.
Yet, that knowledge has never stopped a farmer from sowing.
In this particular case
    he happened to sow grain on four different types of land.
Some grain fell on the foot path across the field.
The seed just sat there on the hard packed ground.
    The birds came and ate it.
Some grain fell on rocky ground.
The top soil was so thin
    there was no chance for the grain to put down roots.
When the sun came up the weak shoots were burnt up.
Then there were thorn bushes around the edge of the field.
The grain that fell amongst them started to grow
    but it was choked out by the thorn bushes.
The fourth type of soil was good.
It was deep and dark and rich in all the right things.
From this soil there was a surprising crop of grain.
The reapers were working overtime to handle it!
    "You see," said Jesus,

    "three quarters of the seed produced nothing!
    One quarter of the seed produced a tremendous harvest.
    Three quarters of the soil supported nothing at all."
A fair warning of what the Church might expect.
    One quarter of the soil gave excellent results.
A strong message of hope to defeat disappointment and despair.
    "There is your answer to the question," said Jesus.
    "There are people who *listen* to what we are saying,
    and who never *hear* a word of it.
    They are case hardened against the Gospel."[2]
Experience teaches us that they
    are both inside and outside the Church.
Those outside the Church are determined to do nothing
    that will alter or change their ways of belief or behaviour.
The people like that inside the Church
    are there for another coat of varnish.
They go away as impervious to the Gospel message
    as they were when they first arrived.
        Which may have been years before.
There are other people who *listen* to what we are saying,
    and who respond a little bit at first.
These people drop out
    when other things seem more important to them
        than trying to live the Gospel and to promote it.
There are some people who *listen* to what we are saying
    and who respond to it despite all sorts of obstacles.
The obstacles may take the shape of the company they keep,
    the ineffective support of their friends,
        or the weak example of other Christians.
Eventually they, too, are forced to admit defeat
    to the opposition to the Gospel all around them.
If these responses were the whole story,
    whether in the Church or in our own lives,
        we would soon give up in despair.
The Good News is what happens
    when the response is positive and long-lasting.

When the response is always developing,
> always growing, however slowly.
More important to every community
than all the people who resist or ignore the Gospel,
> or who drop out when the going gets rough,
>> or who eventually give in to the pressures all around them,
>>> are the people in whose lives the Gospel has taken hold.
These are the people
> whose lives are continually being transformed
>> into the likeness of Jesus Christ.
>>> No matter how long it takes.
No one may compel another person
> to make any one of these different responses to the Gospel.
We make them for ourselves,
> depending on our reaction to the teaching of Jesus.
Anyone who risks sowing grain also risks poor crops.
Anyone who risks preaching, teaching, and living the Gospel
> also risks failure and opposition to it.
That is entirely predictable.
Yet, that should never discourage us from doing it.
Because here, too, there is also
> the realistic expectation of a good harvest.
It is based on the prediction of Jesus
> and the experience of the Church for 2,000 years.
In terms of our *personal* lives as Christians
> this parable provides a model for the way we handle
>> disappointment, discouragement, and despair.
It means, first of all, that we face failure realistically.
We name it for what it is.
Jesus openly admitted his reverses.
> He identified with the disciples' disappointment.
He and they faced failure together.
Nether did they accept all of the blame for all of it.
> Nor should we.
There is no one of us who has escaped failure and discouragement
>> in a variety of ways.

Both in terms of our faith
>and in terms of our personal experience.

Whenever we face failure of whatever kind,
>we don't take all of the blame for it.

In this parable Jesus refused to make himself liable
>for the decisions of other people.

The crowds listening to him on the beach
>were under an obligation to answer for themselves.

The answer, the response, was a matter of *their* decision
>about what to do with the message they heard.

The decision was their own.³
>It is one that not even God could make for them.

This means that they were challenged
>to take responsibility for their own decisions.

To take charge of their own lives.

That is where we are!
>All of us, all of the time.

We are under obligation to decide for ourselves
>*who* or *what* or *where* the centre of our lives is going to be.

The privilege and the responsibility
>for the decisions you make belongs to you!

That was the challenge of Jesus to the people on the beach.

That is always the challenge
>to those of us who are in the Church now.

We are so used to listening,
>to scripture being read,
>>to prayers being offered,
>>>to sermons being preached,
>>>>to promises being made,
>>>>>that we may not *hear* anything any more.

Listening and hearing are very different from one another.
>"Listening is like watching the scenery
>from the window of a fast moving train.
>Hearing is getting off at the station
>and becoming involved in the human struggle."⁴

According to the Gospel,

Jesus expects his followers to get off at the station.
He expects them to do something about the problems
    facing the community and the Church.
This includes their personal problems as well.
Otherwise we are in danger of drowning in discouragement
    and despair, which is so easy to do.
Because of the promise in the parable,
    that God is able to bring an amazing harvest from good soil,
        we never give up trying on behalf of God.
Or on our own behalf either.
That we can still count on God,
    and really believe that we can,
        no matter what the circumstance,
            is the best news we have to hang on to.
The disciples were hypnotized by failures.
The peddlers of despair seemed to have sold their product.
Yet, in that situation,
    despite every evidence to the contrary,
        Jesus pointed instead to the hope of a harvest
            beyond reasonable human expectation.
He pointed to a welcome outcome,
    provided we rely on resources beyond our own,
        and always including our own as well.
God specializes in harvests,
    not crop failures.
In your life and in mine.
Jesus said so.
    We believe it to be true!
                Amen.

1. Peter Rhea Jones, *The Teaching Of The Parables* (Nashville, Tennessee: Broadman Press, 1982). "William Neil put it, 'The farmer does not lose heart although he knows that much of his work will come to nothing.'"

2. Frederick C. Grant, *The Interpreter's Bible*, Vol. VII, Analysis and Exegesis (New York: Abingdon Press, 1951), p. 695-698. The experience of Christian evangelism showed, then as now, that some hearers are, as the Salvation Army has described them — "gospel proof."

3. Emil Brunner, *Sowing And Reaping*, trans. T. Weise (Richmond: John Knox Press, 1954), p. 14. "You are not the rocky ground, the thorny ground or the trodden path; you become one or the other, depending on your reaction to God's Word."

4. Professor Donald MacLeod, "Don't Just Listen, HEAR!" The Princeton Seminary Bulletin, 3.57 (ns., 1980).

Mark 6:6b-13
Ephesians 1:3-10
Amos 7:12-17

What Time Is It?

Today is September 20, 2006.
It is a day during which my wife and I,
    along with many others in Canada and Ireland,
        are dealing with sadness and shock.
The death of The Reverend Professor Raymond Humphries,
    Toronto, Ontario, has saddened us beyond words.
He was a person totally committed to ideas,
   he had outstanding intellect, exceptional wit,
     and with it all a teenage sort of playfulness.
He had been a parish minister and then an academic.
He was an omnivorous reader
    and seemed to remember everything he read.
He quoted English and Latin poetry and prose at will.
    Above all he was a good friend.
Many years ago, Raymond described
    a cartoon he enjoyed
        in one of the Scottish national magazines.
The cartoon was a simple one.
It focused attention on two large signs at the fork of a road.
    On one fork of the road a sign was marked:
        "This Road Leads to Heaven" — there was no one on that
            road.
The second sign read:
    "This Road Leads To A Committee Meeting Where
    We Will Talk About Heaven" — that road was crowded!
Long time members of our Christian communities sense that,
    since the days of their youth, a note of urgency
        seems to be missing from the message of the Church.

They suspect, and their suspicions are well founded,
> that too many of us are on the road to the Committee Meeting,
>> while not enough of us are on the road to heaven.

When we are reminded of these things,
> we know our elders are speaking truth.

Obviously, we cannot recover a feeling of urgency
> merely by pretending to live in the past.

Unless we reach out our hands and raise our voices in mission,
> we shall pass out and away from the scene.

As we should deserve to do.

The mission of the Church in these early years of the twenty-first
> century has been blunted from its increasing contact
>> with humanism and secularism.

By contrast, the Church flourished in the second century
> from increasing persecution and martyrdom.

According to this Gospel, Jesus first trained his disciples,
> and later sent them out in pairs to test their training.

During their first skirmish with the world,
> they remained close to him in terms of distance and time.

When they did as they had been sent out to do,
> they hurried back to report on their success or failure.

The nation believed itself to be the People of God.

Given such a conviction,
> it might have been expected to be self-conscious of its
>> responsibilities and active in the pursuit of them.

Rather, it appeared like a Great Bear that had been anaesthetized.

It appeared to be so drugged that anyone could play with it
> or humiliate it as he or she pleased without danger.

It had to recover its senses,
> realize its caged captivity, and move aggressively
>> against its spiritual enemies.

To accomplish this task, Jesus sent out his disciples in pairs.

They were to speak with anyone who would listen to them.

The disciples realized that time had been wasted.

Too much time had been spent in a Committee Room.

Not enough time had been spent at the Financial and Educational
> headquarters in Jerusalem.

Then, too, the busy marketplaces had been ignored.
In Mark's Gospel the stress is on hurry!
In his Gospel he uses the word "immediately" over forty times.
In other words, there is no time to waste.
According to Mark, the disciples were aware
    that at any time the clock might strike midnight.
When that happened all hope of doing
    what ought to have been done was impossible.
It was from that conviction they spoke to their neighbours,
    their friends, and to strangers without exception.
The New Testament writers are conscious of the thoroughness
    with which Jesus understood human nature.
We see it once again in this first mission of the disciples.
One of the best ways to learn something is to teach it.
It is one of the best pedagogical methodologies.
The late Professor George B. Caird used to tell his classes
that he was taught the Greek language
    "by the time-honoured method of teaching it to someone else."
Similarly, the disciples who had been taught about God by Jesus
    taught others what they had been told and believed.
They had been witnesses to certain miraculous events.
They believed that what they had seen
    were demonstrations of the awesome power of God in the world.
In order to make these experiences convincing for others
    they had to leave the Committee Meetings and take their places
        as evangelists for God.
It is when you attempt to share them with someone else
    that your convictions and experiences are made real to you.
Actually, there are biblical writers who teach that *unless* you
    share your convictions with other people, or attempt to,
        they mean nothing much to you!
How that is done is an issue for each Christian to discover.
Pope John XXIII commented:
    "The first task of the discipleship today
    is to make Christians of those already inside the Church."
What he had to say to his own Church

is equally applicable to the Reformed Churches as well.
This was the method used by Jesus in the mission described by Mark.
His disciples were sent to their own people.
He sent them to people who believed in God in a formal way.
People who came to say their prayers.
People who supported with their offerings their places of worship.
The disciples were first sent to "religious" people.
The mission to the Gentiles, the pagans, came later.
The message they had was brief and to the point.
It concerned the Reign of God:
    where it was and to whom it had come.
The Kingdom of God is an expression for the Reign of God
    in the lives of men, women, and children.
The Reign of God in our lives comes about
    when we see in the person of Jesus the truth about God.
Then to give ourselves to the service of the truth.
The disciples had caught from Jesus the truth about God
    for our living and for our dying;
        for our despair and for our hopes,
            for our doubts and our believing,
                for our sinfulness, and for the forgiveness of God.
According to the New Testament,
    when they spoke about Jesus the disciples taught simply:
        "This is what he *did* for me and for many others.
        This is what he *said* to me."
The most effective sort of preaching that anyone may do,
    inside or outside the Church, happens when one person says to
        another "This is what he means to me!"
It is as if a friend were to catch up with you on a street
    and say to you with urgency:
        "I cannot wait another minute to tell you of something
            wonderful and personal that has happened to me!"
The message of the mission is that something great
    had happened in Jerusalem and that something great
        may happen wherever you live.
The Reign of God has come to both places.

If there is in either one of them a person
    in whose life there reigns the Lord of all Life.
The message of the mission is an intensely personal one.
Those who hear will react in either a positive or a negative way.
The Christian message was at first
    understood to mean a "separatist" movement.
When people spoke about the Kingdom of God, the Reign of God,
    those who heard it thought he was speaking about something
        like a new state of Quebec.
As a consequence of this misunderstanding,
    people followed him hoping that he would rid them
        of their hated occupation powers.
These same people later left him in disappointment.
We want every story to have a happy ending, a good ending.
We would prefer to have the story of the first Christian mission
    end in success.
Unhappily, it did not!
Jesus regarded it as a failure.
So much so that he moved to another area of the country
    where the people were more receptive.
He had been a popular person in Galilee.
However, the popularity was barely skin deep.
It was so shallow it did not touch the lives of those
    who found him an interesting Teacher and a strong personality.
The people remained deaf to the Gospel,
    they ignored his call to a new life.
Speaking of this sort of reaction to the message,
    Jesus said it reminded him of sulky children refusing
        to join in games or dances without regard
            for anything done for them.
He left them to their own devices after first acquitting himself
    of his responsibility for them.
Jesus is saying that although we are not responsible to God
    for *results*, we are responsible to God for *efforts*.
He is saying that a disciple must not batter out his or her own
    life against a wall that will not be breached.

He must seek a place where breaching is possible
>and not to give up the mission.
When one door closes in our faces,
>we prepare to knock on another one.
If one town refuses to listen to us,
>there are other towns that will.
According to Mark, we remember all the while that time
>is so short it cannot be wasted in a housekeeper sort of discipleship.
There is more to be done than merely passing the time of day!
In 2006, the aim of the mission is the same as it was
>during the time of the disciples.
In our day it is to shake up the Church from its lethargy.
To do so in time for the Church to realize much remains to be done.
Our message to the congregation, the community,
>the world is the one Jesus gave to his people.
It is a message that tells us about God and about us,
>about life and about death, about hope and about despair.
The mission will not always be successful.
>Success is not our responsibility.
We are to be faithful to the end of our discipleship,
>and to leave the results in the hands of God.
>>Amen.

(One summer afternoon, many years ago, while the minister of The First Presbyterian Church Montreal, I tried street-corner evangelism. It was a challenging experience and, try as I might, I was unable to share my convictions with anyone else. That does not mean everyone who tries such an approach is destined to be a failure!)

Mark 6:12-13
cf. James 5:13-18

Preach, Teach, And Heal

One evening some thirty years ago, a young woman
    was ordained to the ministry in a Reformed Church.
After the service of ordination was over
    her parents said they had been deeply moved
        by what they had seen and heard that evening.
"What a wonderful service,"
    they said to the Moderator of Presbytery.
"May we have a copy of it to read at our leisure?"
The young woman who had just been ordained said:
    "I have the service in my Book of Common Order.
    And I must read it again as well.
    I hardly heard a word that was said this evening.
    I was very nervous."
That was a great pity!
Because the things that had been said and done that evening
    are meant to last a lifetime.
As the young woman knelt before the Presbytery,
and while the ministers held their hands on her head,
the Moderator of Presbytery had used phrases
from an ancient prayer of ordination.
In it the Moderator asked for the gift of the Holy Spirit
    to inspire the young woman in her preaching,
    to correct her in her teaching,
    and to strengthen her in her healing.
In the Service of Ordination
    these petitions are summed up in these words:
        "Garrison her with Thy peace,
        that she may be a maker of peace

and a healer of people in their anxiety, strife, and
greed, their sorrow, pain, and guilt."
The intention of that prayer is, of course,
in obedience to the teaching of Jesus.
According to the Gospels,
Jesus instructed his followers to preach, teach, and heal.
The Early Church proclaimed the Gospel of Jesus Christ.
It taught the peculiar convictions of the Christian community.
It healed the sick — in body, mind, and spirit.
We need read only the Acts of the Apostles
to realize that these things were done
as three separate aspects of the Christian ministry.
With the passage of time
the Church concentrated on preaching and teaching,
which always included the celebration of the Sacraments.
The healing aspect of the Christian ministry,
which is the most demanding aspect of the three,
was allowed to deteriorate and, in most cases, to disappear.[1]
Yet, we are reminded, whenever we read the New Testament,
that the Christian ministry is at best partially complete
when it obeys only parts, and those the easiest parts,
of our Lord's instructions.
Preach, teach, and heal!
Those were the instructions of Jesus
as remembered and obeyed by the early Christian community.
"Greater things than these shall you do!"
That was the promise of Jesus
to those who were faithful to his teaching and example.
The preaching of the Gospel,
the teaching of the distinctive convictions of the Church,
these things, in one way or other,
the people of God have done.
The healing aspect of the Christian ministry
has been neglected — almost without embarrassment.
"Heal the sick,"
not when it is convenient or when you feel like it,

    but as a regular part of the ministry of every Christian.[2]
What we think of the healing ministry of the Church
  really depends on what we think about the power of God.
Is it or is it not at work in the world
  through the Holy Spirit of the Risen Christ?
Is it a present reality or is it not?
  Is it effective or is it impotent?
What we think about the healing ministry of the Church
  depends *not* on your faith or on mine.
Our measure of faith is never enough.
It depends rather on our faith in the power of God,
  that, through Christ, God may and does heal
    those whose wounds are both seen and unseen.
We live in an age when we may benefit
  from all the miracles of modern medicine
    and the skill of highly trained physicians.
The Christian Church supports modern medicine
  and twenty-first-century physicians as much today
    as it has supported medicine and medical people
      at any time in its history.
One of the differences at the moment is that the Church
has come again to realize that it has resources at its disposal,
for the wholeness of humanity,
that will always be denied to medicine of any age.[3]
Sometimes we are in the embarrassing position
  of having to be asked by Christian physicians and nurses
    to do the very things we ought to have been doing all along.
When a Christian ministers to someone in distress,
when he or she prays with and for such a person,
when one's hands are laid on the person in compassion,
and perhaps the person is anointed with oil,
such a Christian is merely doing what Jesus did,
what the apostles did in the name of Jesus,
what the early Christians did in obedience to Jesus,
and what we are commanded to do in the New Testament.[4]
Do you ever wonder on what basis Christians decide
  to follow certain New Testament instructions

and to ignore others?
Think for a moment about some of them.
We are instructed to love and forgive one another.
We are provided with examples of how serious a matter this is.
We are instructed to baptize in the Name of God:
    Father, Son, and Holy Spirit.
To celebrate the Lord's Supper when we come together in worship.
To wash one another's feet as Jesus did in the Upper Room.
What about the command to love one another
    as we are loved by God?
Or the necessity to forgive one another
    as we would like to be forgiven?
When was the last time
    you either gave or received love or forgiveness
        within the Christian community?
When was the last time you attended a meeting
    and came away from it
        with an awareness of love and forgiveness for one
            another?[5]
Or has it ever happened at all?
We celebrate the sacraments of Baptism and Holy Communion,
    and we leave out the Foot Washing.
On what basis?
The problem is not a shortage of water — not normally.
Foot Washing is a Sacrament based on humility,
    and humility is often in short supply.
Preach, teach, and heal, instructed Jesus.
We have all sorts of persons who preach and teach.
We always have had.
The healing is left out.
    On what basis?
Certainly the things the apostles said and did
    are not difficult ones to remember or perform.
Healing, as an example, is surrounded by prayer.
Prayer has never been an easy matter.
The more clever we imagine ourselves to be,

the more difficult it is to pray.
Remember the New Testament story
   of the disciples and their failure to heal a person?
How Jesus was successful in the face of their failure?
The difference, Jesus said,
   boils down to the practice of prayer and fasting.
We are not much given to fasting.
   We have not much practice and no instruction in it.
      We go to Weight Watchers instead!
The same might almost be said about prayer.
   Most of us are not much good at that either.
      No one teaches us any more how to pray.
         Or how to persist in prayer.
To the best of my knowledge few in our colleges
   teach our people in training for ministry how to pray.
      Neither are they asked whether they pray!
Yet there is nothing more basic
   to the Christian life and ministry than the practice of prayer.
It is prayer, first of all things,
   that lies at the basis of the ministry of healing.
The congregations in which healing takes place
   are communities in which there are people who love one another
      enough to pray regularly for those in need.
When a minister in these congregations is concerned for healing
   the prayers of the parish give him or her the strength
      and the authority to proclaim the healing power of God
         in Jesus Christ.
The ministry of healing is a spiritual adventure
   into unknown territory for the most of us.
In that way it is quite like the experience of faith itself.
It is a spiritual adventure
   into territory you cannot see or touch or understand
      until you take Christ at his Word and obey him.
The follower of Jesus who proclaims the healing power of God,
who blesses, who loves, who anoints, who forgives,
all in the Name of his or her Lord,

is like the preacher who, having done everything human to convince
or convert, is then content to leave the rest to the mysterious
power of God.
Certainly such a one makes no claim for her or his own powers.
We cannot retrace the steps of the first Christians.
Even if we could, it would do little to change or heal us.
At the same time, there are some things in our day
    which are precisely the same as they were
        when the first Christians were alive and active.
In our pulpits and in our pews
    there is hatred, pride, guilt, worry, hurt,
        fear, depression, jealousy, loneliness,
            the need to forgive and to be forgiven.
There is sickness of all kinds.
    There is evil masking as good.
According to the Gospel of Mark these were matters
    high on the priority list of Jesus.
Jesus expected they would be high on our list as well.
The expectations of Jesus
    and our performance of them are often far apart.
A Christian is someone called by God
    to preach, teach, and heal in the name of Christ.
These are three equal aspects of our ministry to one another.
These three aspects belong together,
    or our ministry is incomplete.
        Maybe even disobedient!
Let us pray then that the Church of Jesus Christ
    will recover the healing ministry of her Lord.
So that more and more she may bring
    healing, wholeness, and peace to her people.[6]
        Amen.

1. Dennis Linn, S.J., & Matthew Linn, S.J., *Healing Life's Hurts: Healing Memories Through Five Stages Of Forgiveness* (New York: Paulist Press, 1978). This is a book I have found exceedingly helpful.

2. Mary E. Peterman, *Healing: A Spiritual Adventure* (Philadelphia: Fortress Press, 1979). This excellent little book was recommended by Pastor Don Stroh, many years ago, when he was Pastor of Zion Lutheran Church in Stratford, Ontario.

3. Francis MacNutt, O.P., *Healing* (Notre Dame, Indiana: Ave Maria Press, 1985). The cover note describes this book as "The first comprehensive Catholic book on healing by the foremost authority on the healing ministry in the Roman Catholic Church today."

4. Francis MacNutt, O.P., *The Power To Heal* (Notre Dame, Indiana: Ave Maria Press, 1977). An excellent text on the subject.

5. Bernie S. Siegel, M.D., *Peace, Love & Healing* (New York: Harper & Row, Publishers, 1990). This splendid book is by the well-known author of *Love, Medicine & Miracles*.

6. Lewis B. Smedes, *Forgive & Forget: Healing The Hurts We Don't Deserve* (New York: Pocket Books, 1984). Rabbi Harold Kushner, author of *When Bad Things Happen To Good People*, writes of this book: "A warm, wise, and helpful book ... I know that many people will be as helped by it as I was."

See also commentaries on the text.

Mark 6:30-34
Hebrews 3:7-4, 11
Exodus 23:10-12

A Vital Balance

From Castelgondolfo, the Pope's summer residence in Italy,
Benedict XVI issued an interesting comment on work and rest.
On Sunday, August 20th, 2006, he said:
"Too much work can be bad for you."[1]
He quoted from the works of St. Bernard of Clairvaux,
who lived in the eleventh and twelfth centuries.
"We have to guard ourselves, the Saint observed, from the
dangers of excessive activity, regardless of the office one
holds, because too many concerns can often lead to
hardness of heart," the Pope said.
"This warning is valid for every type of job,
even those concerned with the government of the Church."
The 79-year-old Pope Benedict noted that the Saint had written
to the Pope of the day, Eugene III,
warning him of the dangers of working too hard.
Pope Benedict said one should always make room
for "prayer and contemplation."
Doubtless Pope Benedict was thinking of the crushing load
he has to bear as the Spiritual Head of a large part
of the Christian world.
This raises the question:
"How much time to you have for yourself each year
and what do you do with it?"
This question lies as the basis of a statement
from a committee in the Department of Health
in the United States on the amount of leisure time available
to many North Americans.
For instance, the report comments that any person

who has Saturday and Sunday free each week, plus two weeks
of annual holidays and the other civic and religious holy
days, receives annually about 120 days free from work.
This is equivalent to about four months' leisure time,
or about one third of one's life.
The average school age person does somewhat better,
when you consider the annual summer break from classes,
plus the weekends and other holidays specific to school
education.
In other words, it appears that many people,
but by no means everyone, have the equivalent of four months
each year not spent at regular work.
There are some work places where these statistics do not apply.
Farmers, fisher folk, and other necessary service people,
have few opportunities for relief from work.
The same is true for the thousands of people, both young and old,
who work for minimum wage in the coffee shops and service
stations in Canada and the United States.
The wages in some of these situations are scandalously low![2]
The people who work in well known chains of coffee shops and
fast food places must struggle to have two jobs to make ends meet.
One of the disappointing features of the report
concerns the use made of free time.
Many people do little or nothing with it.
Even worse, many people fuss and fret
until the holidays are over and they are back at work.
Medical people have often commented on the fact that people have
headaches on the weekend which disappear as soon as
Monday morning comes and they are back at work.
There are other people who cannot or will not rest at any time.
Their lives are a part of the human traffic jam in the world.
Life for them is often confused and disorganized.
Some of them are never satisfied that they have done enough work.
If they should be seen to take some relaxation,
they are so overcome with guilt that they wear their bodies
to a frazzle and their nerves to a ragged edge.
Every person needs some time when we may stop

and let our systems catch up with our activity.
Health is always more important than money in the bank.
It is more important than academic success,
> though few academics believe it enough to take it seriously.

Within the Church we might expect that people would reach
> the vital balance between activity and rest more naturally
>> than their opposite numbers in modern secular and pagan society.

Unhappily, this is not the case.
North American Protestantism
> is almost a religion of constant activity.

Some congregations refer to their buildings as "the plant."
This is a clue to their attitude about it.
When asked how he integrated new members in the congregation,
> one minister replied:

"Get them busy right away and try to keep them that way."
The activity of Church members may not have anything
> to do with responsible discipleship in the world.

Even when a congregation intends to do what it is meant to be
> doing, there are wonderful people whose lives are sucked into a
>> whirlpool where there is no time for rest, thought, or prayer.

The temptation for Christians to keep busy is great.
Once involved in the excitement of discipleship, an excitement that
> is self-perpetuating, one is carried along with it.

For this reason, a disciple may keep going for long hours,
> seven days a week, on the exhilaration of meeting human need.

He or she may move on the happiness of sharing experiences
> or watching a tortured soul finding its way to healing,
>> wholeness, and peace.

There are times when it is difficult, if not impossible,
> for a Christian to stop or even to slow down.

This was precisely the situation following the first session of
> practical training for the disciples.

They came back to Jesus excited by their experiences in society.
In Jesus' name they had healed the sick, done some teaching about
> God, and both watched and listened to the results.

In their rush to tell Jesus the whole story of their varied

experiences, each man competed with the other
    to tell his story first.
They had been carried along
    by the excitement of their discipleship.
Nonetheless, Jesus had noticed
    the tell-tale signs of fatigue and exhaustion.
They had gone without proper food or rest
    and now they were in need of both.
Someone tried to prepare a meal.
There was so much interruption he had to abandon his attempts.
The bystanders wanted to share in the experiences
    and to receive some attention, as well.
Eventually, Jesus gathered the disciples into a boat.
They rowed away to a place where it would be quiet.
It was a lonely place where people could think and talk at leisure.
It was bad enough not to have a moment even to eat a sandwich.
Yet, that is a commonplace situation today.
Normally, we have little time for living in its deepest sense
    and almost *no* time for reading and thinking about the important
        decisions that shape our lives.
A long-time retired medical doctor,
    once an important medical person in his city, cannot rest.
Three times a week he calls the General Hospital
    to ask whether the hospital has been calling for him.
A lifetime of meeting human need will not let him relax
    and enjoy a well earned rest.
Surely, after the pattern of Jesus and the disciples in this text,
the Creator intended a vital balance between the activity of a
Christian in society and her or his relaxation and recreation.
The balance is vital to the health and happiness of the individual.
Without it a person is unable to play a role
    in bringing in the Reign of God in the world.
There are few of us who would complain
    that we do too much work as a Christian disciple.
Most of us need to do much more than we do.
It is the rush and bustle and confusion

in which our work is done that kills.
We find it difficult to take seriously
    the balance Jesus showed between contact with people
        and withdrawal from the presence of people.
He did not give anyone the impression that there was virtue
    in wearing oneself to a health crisis.
Actually, he illustrated quite the opposite approach
    to responsibility.
A surprising number of references in the New Testament may be
indicated to illustrate his quest for privacy from people and his
search for a quiet time with God.
This pattern of discipleship is the one commended by Benedict XVI.
This has been the pattern of deeply spiritual people
    who were also wholesome, healthy individuals.
The rhythm of life should alternate between meeting with God
    and serving the needs of the people of God.
The scriptures, both Old and New Testaments, teach that if we are
too busy to allow our strength to return through re-creation,
we are also too busy to serve God with the best we have.
The Christian ought to take good care of his/her body
    because it is the home of the Spirit of God.
No other person but the Christian believes
    about the human body as we do.
If this is so, and we believe it is, it becomes a primary duty,
    as well as common sense, to take reasonable care of our health
        and strength.
It then becomes a sinful thing to let our nervous health suffer
    or our physical condition deteriorate.
It is blasphemous to say at a grave side:
    "The Lord gives and the Lord takes away"
when in many cases it was quite plainly the deceased
who took himself or herself away.
There is no vacation from Christian discipleship,
    nor ought there be.
There is a vital balance between the activity of a Christian

as a disciple and withdrawal in preparation
for more intelligent activity.
The use of our free time, whether on annual vacation
or on a weekend, ought to be so chosen that afterward
we will live and work for God at peak performance.
Once upon a time in the long ago,
"The disciples returned to Jesus and told him all
that they had done and taught. And he said to them:
'Come away by yourselves to a lonely place, and rest a
while.' For many were coming and going, and they had no
leiure even to eat. And they went away in a boat to a
lonely place by themselves."
Amen.

---

1. Reuters News Agency. Reported in the *Vancouver Sun*, 21st August, 2006.

2. The people who work in well known chains of coffee shops and fast food places must struggle to have two jobs to make ends meet.

Mark 7:1-8, 14-26
James 1:19-25
Deuteronomy 4:1-8

A Problem Of Pollution

In terms of environmental concerns,
    much has happened since 1971.
In that year, Canada appointed its first Minister responsible
    for the protection and preservation of the environment.
At the time, concern for pollution of the air, land, and sea
    did not register very high with the average Canadian.
Until that time no one seemed to be taking the problem of
    pollution at all seriously.
Nothing in 1971 could have prepared the public
    for worldwide concerns about pollution 35 years later.
During the last months of 2005,
    Canada hosted the largest ever International Conference
        on the problems of environmental pollution of every kind.
At the moment all sorts of people are concerned about pollution;
    its many sources, its devastating effects, its arrest
        and possible control.[1]
These people include professional conservationists, certainly,
    and also part-time conservationists who may be full-time
        teachers, doctors, lawyers, shop people, and stage celebrities.
Environmental pollution has characteristics we can see,
    smell, and some we may touch and taste.
We see smog, like a great grey-blue cap, suspended over
    our major North American cities.
We see and sometimes smell dead fish floating on the surface
    of lakes, rivers, and streams.
We may taste foods that have been affected in some way,
    or we may touch leaves that are dried and dead
        as a result of the poisons in the air.
Environmental pollution is often obvious to our senses.

That is just as well.
    Otherwise we might not recognize it for what it is.
It is a concern that will be with us for many years to come.
The sources, as well as the results, of this form of pollution,
    are always from the *outside*.
The pollution comes from something being poured into the sea,
    the air, or torn from the earth.
There is also pollution of a personal kind as well.
It, too, takes a variety of forms
    and it has a number of expressions.
Unlike the pollution of the environment,
    personal pollution has been a concern for thinking people
        for many thousands of years.
It had been a major concern for our spiritual ancestors,
    the Hebrew people.[2]
It was also a preoccupation for certain elements in Greek culture,
    elements that later influenced Christianity.
Both the Hebrew and Greek societies believed that personal
    pollution, like environmental pollution,
        had come from outside influences.
Therefore, any remedies were imposed from the outside as well.
Most often they began with an attempt to reform
    the behaviour of the people who were personally polluted.
In some instances, rules and regulations were organized
    for better physical health, which is certainly important.
Reform movements would demand complete loyalty
    to physical exercise and a basic healthy diet.
The result would change the appearance of people.
They looked healthier and stronger, for so they were.
Otherwise, they were not different people in any basic way.
Other attempts were made to reform people
    through the stimulation of their minds.
They were encouraged to follow specific mental exercises.
The sayings of the wise were discussed or debated.
The normal result was a small change
    in the intellectual interests of a small number of people.
Those with lazy minds had to work hard

if they were to become alert and interested.
Once in condition, these people came to enjoy a discussion
 as others might enjoy a race or a game.
However, these people, too, were not transformed
 in anything but a superficial way.
The modern curse of the drug culture, a curse in every way,
 began long, long ago as an attempt to release the human mind
  for fellowship with the mind of God.
The users became tranquilized.
Some experienced what is called "mind expansion."
They spoke only of failure to gain insight
 into anything significant about God or man.
Many users experienced only depression
 in their so-called search for a moral and mental clean-up.
In 2006, they are looking for nothing more than a "high."
Our spiritual ancestors, the Hebrew people,
sought to clean-up the People of God, by supplying them
with elaborate rules and regulations for living.
The people were taught to wash their hands in a certain way.
 To eat only designated foods.
  To use only certain dishes.
   To have social dealings only with their own people.
The more difficult the regulations, the better they felt.
We know, from personal experience, how much easier it is to
 indulge in distractions as an excuse for actual work.
In terms of dealing with personal pollution,
 our spiritual ancestors were hardly more successful
  than were their neighbours.
The preoccupation with rules and regulations did little more
 than produce self-righteousness and pride.
They could see the effects of personal pollution, just as we do.
There is no grouping of people so small that it is without
 slander, the destruction of reputation or character.
There is no grouping of people that is without murder,
 a total disregard for the lives and rights of other people.
Or the serious matter of adultery,

a desire to have a person who is committed to someone else.
The overall disregard for God in life so that people are treated
like things, and things are treated as people ought to be.
Jesus listed twelve consequences of personal pollution.
Doubtless, he knew of as many more. His society certainly did.
He called together his disciples and taught them, saying:
"Hear this, and make no mistake what I am saying.
The problem is one of personal pollution.
We are agreed on that much.
We disagree on the source of the pollution
and, therefore, we disagree on the measures to be taken
to deal with it.
You want to regard the source of pollution as coming from
the outside, things like food and water.
Bad company, pornographic literature, films, and web sites.
Obscene telephone calls, X-rated movies, and a thousand
other things."
Jesus went on to teach his listeners:
"You would like to cure the disease,
to counteract the poison, to stop the pollution
by imposing something from the outside.
Perhaps an absorbing concern for the institution
itself. Or boring yourself to death in meetings,
religious or otherwise, that are without point or purpose.
It may be by doing good deeds, or by reminding others
of the good they ought to be doing.
It won't work!
It won't work because it cannot work.
The things that defile a person, man, woman, or child,
are the things that come from deep within that person.
What we see and experience are the expressions in attitude
or behaviour of the inner problem.
The source of the problem lies within our spirits.
It begins inside, although it never ends there."
The human heart is like a clever chemist gone berserk.
It distills a terrible poison.

Then pours it from a full beaker into every area of life.
You may help a person appear in good health,
> but it won't change her/his heart.

You may improve someone's mind,
> but that won't transform his/her spirit.

You may distract attention from basic issues by forcing folk to concentrate on trivia.
However, the Church knows that distraction is never the way to deal with personal pollution.[3]
Long, long ago, perhaps 4,000 years ago,
> one of the ancestors of Jesus felt as Jesus did about personal pollution.

Preparing for a complete change in his life,
> looking for a transformation of the human spirit
>> he spoke to God in these words:
>>> "Create in me a clean heart, O God, and renew a right Spirit within me."

It is just that simple.
> It is just that difficult.
>> Amen.

1. Mike Blanchard, *Vancouver Sun*, 14th August, 2006, p. 14. "Canada is ranked as one of the least environmentally friendly countries, placing seventeenth in a survey of the world's richest nations."

2. Samuel Tobias Lachs, *Rabbinic Commentary On The New Testament: The Gospel Of Matthew, Mark, And Luke* (Hoboken, New Jersey: KTAV Publishing House, Inc., 1987), p. 246. "The disciples of Jesus ate without washing their hands, that is, they defied the tradition of the Pharisees and their decrees in which they declared that every Jew was in a state of impurity and hence before eating had to wash his hands. For this the Pharisees reproached Jesus ... this passage must have been written by the evangelist after the destruction of the Temple and projected back to Jesus and his disciples."

3. Father Shay. *Reflections From PREDA* (Philippines #269). A column on the destruction of the earth, of the animal and human species, leading to eventual extinction. In face of all this, Father Shay endorses a spiritual turnaround, what the Greek text calls a turning from sin and a turning to God. See www.preda.org.

Mark 8:27-38
James 2:14-18
Isaiah 50:4-9

A Difference Of Opinion

Some memories of the past
    are as present today as the experience itself.
It is "as if" certain experiences and particular persons
    have never been absent from us.
One of these, amongst many, of people and experiences
is the memory of an Ecumenical Service of Worship in the long ago.
The Guest Preacher was from Halifax, the late Canon Puxley,
    who was, at the time, the President of the University of Kings College.
He preached an excellent sermon.
A sermon that lingers in the minds of some of us
    who were there at the time.
Amongst other things,
    he spoke of the goals we set for ourselves,
        and of the goals other people set for us.
Rarely are the goals the same,
    either in quality or in kind.
Often they differ on what it is that constitutes
    a successful career or a promising future.
This sort of difference of opinion
    is a familiar experience.
There are all sorts of people who live and work
    in close association with one another for years.
They take for granted, they assume,
    that they share in common the same goals and values.
Suddenly, something happens to make them realize
    they had never known what was going on
        in the hearts and minds of each other.

The discovery may come as a complete surprise,
    whether it takes place within a family,
        amongst close friends, within a congregation,
        or a college community!
Something of the sort happened between Jesus and his disciples.
When it did, the relationship between all of them
    was never the same again.
Together they had shared similar experiences,
    including physical discomfort and inconvenience.
There were times when, as Jesus predicted, they were as uncertain of their welcome in a town or village as they were unfortunate in their living and travel arrangements.
The disciples kept hoping for better circumstances
    when Jesus was given the recognition he deserved.
They had dreams of comfort,
    of a secure place in society, of positions of influence,
        and of reflected glory.
One day Jesus took a poll amongst his disciples.
In the first instance, he wanted to know the popular opinion,
    the opinion on the street, concerning his identity.
The answers he was given were complimentary ones.
Some people believed him to be John the Baptist come back to life.
Other people saw him as an Elijah figure back from the dead.
There were those, too, who thought of him
    as one of the old-style prophets.
A man who had emerged with a direct message
    concerning political and personal morality.
In any case, the consensus of popular opinion
    is that he was a prophet.
Which prophet was uncertain.
Then, he asked the disciples for their opinion.
Peter, answering for himself and his colleagues, said:
    "You are the Christ," "You are the Messiah."[1]
Surely, that is what you might have expected him to say.
That would seem to have been the answer
    for which Jesus was waiting.

No sooner had it been given than we realize
    it was not the right answer.
        It was not a confession of faith, at all!
It had been a serious misunderstanding.
It was a misunderstanding because it was based on what the
    disciples themselves were looking for in a Messiah.[2]
It was, Jesus knew, an answer bound up with such things
as religious privilege, political power, and material prosperity.
The answer was both right and wrong!
Jesus was, and is, indeed the Christ, the Messiah,
    yet a Christ more different from their expectations
        than could possibly be imagined.
He began at once to correct their misunderstanding
    of who he is in terms not of triumph and privilege,
        but in terms of rejection, arrest, humiliation, and death.
The disciples were scandalized!
They reacted in shock, just as we might have done.
Peter scolded Jesus, in surprise and anger.[3]
He and his fellows could not believe
    that the way of God for Christ should involve
        the complete reversal of their expectations.
The extent of their misunderstanding was so enormous
    that Jesus ordered them out of his sight!
Have you ever held seemingly unshakeable opinions,
or particularly strong convictions on matters important to you,
only to be shown you have been completely mistaken in them?
If you have, you may imagine something
    of the confusion and shock of the disciples.
In a complete reversal of the values they prized,
    of the hopes they held, Jesus outlined, in plain language,
        what is involved in following him:
            "If any person would be my disciple, let him follow me
            by denying himself and taking up his cross."
The goals Jesus had set for himself and the goals
    the disciples had set for him were not the same!
In our society, the people who are popularly envied are those

who have gathered about them the most obvious symbols of
success in financial, political, or social terms.
The individual symbol of the successful life
is presumed to be the "the person who has everything."
Every influence in our culture encourages us
to become such a person.
The attitude necessary to attaining that goal,
or even a modest version of it,
is one of preoccupation with ourselves.
A serious preoccupation with oneself
may determine the friendships that are fostered,
the connections that are cultivated,
and the manner in which careers are planned.
These are not unusual personal attitudes.
These are the accepted standards of behaviour in a secular society.
However, if a person wants to become a follower of Jesus,
and, mind you, no one may force that decision on anyone else,
then the accepted standards are re-evaluated.
The popular values are reversed.
The first call on the one who *willingly* wants to follow Jesus
is to deny oneself as the centre of his or her life.
A preoccupation with ourselves, in whatever form,
means closing ourselves off from God as the centre of life,
and from other people as well, whoever they are.
To deny yourself is to turn your back on the idea
that you are the most important person in the world.
It is not an easy matter, nor is it something that, once done,
is afterward valid for all time.
Christ asks his followers that they turn away
from one set of values and accept, *willingly*,
another one in its place.
According to Jesus,
the most precious thing in the world is your life!
Your life is as precious to God as it is to you.
There is nothing in the world of material, financial, or social
success that is worth a person's life. Nothing!

It is a poor bargain that gains everything the world can possibly
 offer at the cost of one's physical and spiritual life.
Yet, in following Jesus, it may be as necessary for you
 as it was for him, to shoulder the cross and go with it
  to its inevitable conclusion.
Your willingness to make the final sacrifice, if need be,
 does not mean that life in the Church is cheap.
It does mean that to follow Jesus
 is to become involved in a serious enterprise.
It is not something that may be *required* of you,
 by anyone or anything else.
It must be a voluntary act on your part,
 just as free as was the decision to follow Christ
  in the first place.
We need to be assured that the one decision
 involves other ones as well.
Those who fall in behind Jesus, on his terms,
 travel a road strewn with temptation and distraction.
The temptation, I think, is chiefly to follow at a distance,
 with the appearance of following Christ,
  while all the time returning to a preoccupation
   with one's self as the centre of life.
The distractions take our attention away from
 facing those issues in which great sacrifice,
  even martyrdom, may be involved.
By ourselves, it is simply not possible
 to measure up to the demands of Christian discipleship.
The great encouragement in all this
 is that following Christ is never solely our own doing.
It is the gift of God!
It is God who enables us to resolve, voluntarily,
 to reverse the direction of our attention.
It is God who givs us the will to deny ourselves,
 and to go the limit, if need be,
because of the integrity of the Gospel,
 and of our commitment to it.

In this Gospel account, Jesus is uncompromising
in his demands on discipleship.
To quote from Kierkegaard:
"Woe to the person who smoothly, flirtatiously, commandingly,
convincingly preaches some soft sweet something which is
supposed to be Christianity."[4]
God comes into our lives
as wonderfully and as powerfully as love.
You know what that is like!
When you are in love, it seems that your life,
which you have given to someone else,
is given back to you in a way you hardly recognize as your own.
Just as that experience may change and shape you most wonderfully,
just so the experience of God in your life transforms it.
The experience of God in your life enables it to meet
all the new demands made upon it
as a follower of Jesus Christ our Lord.[5]

"Take Up Thy Cross" the Saviour said
"If thou wouldst my disciple be;
Deny thyself, the world forsake
And humbly follow after me."
Amen.

1. Eduard Schweizer, *The Good News According To Mark*, trans. Donald H. Madvig (Atlanta: John Knox Press, 1970), pp. 164ff. The discussion by Schweizer of this passage is one of many and is one of the best.

2. One of the principal themes in the Gospel of Mark is the misunderstanding of the disciples and of the public. He is the Master Teacher because of his role in having often to correct the mistaken ideas of his identity by those who followed him. In this way his Gospel is unique amongst the Synoptic Gospels.

   Frederick C. Grant, *The Gospel According To Mark, Introduction And Exegesis Interpreter's Bible Vol. VII* (New York: Abingdon Press, 1951), p. 768. "Since in biblical usage the first and last days are included, 'three days' is equivalent to 'after two days' ... which is our way of reckoning ... 'after three days' means only, in biblical language, after a brief interval."

   Samuel Tobias Lachs, *A Rabbinic Commentary On The New Testament: The Gospels Of Matthew, Mark And Luke* (Hoboken, New Jersey: KTAV Publishing House, Inc., 1987). "This tradition is in a rabbinic passage that the dead rise from the grave on the third day is based on an interpretation of Hosea 6:2."

3. Mark Galli, *Jesus, Mean And Wild: The Unexpected Love Of An Untameable God* (Grand Rapids, Michigan: Baker Books, 2006), p. 124f.

4. Soren Kierkegaard, "The Offense," in *Provocations: Spiritual Writings of Kierkegaard*, comp. and ed. Charles E. Moore (Farmington, Pennsylvania: Plough Publishing House, 1999), pp. 171-172.

5. W. R. Telford, *The Theology Of The Gospel Of Mark* (Cambridge, Massachusetts: University Press, 1999, reprinted 2003), see pp. 217ff for a splendid discussion of the contemporary significance of Mark.

Mark 8:34-35 (27-35)
James 2:14-18
Isaiah 50:4-9

Speculating In Futures

In 1990, plus or minus a year or two,
 a representative of an investment company
  conducted a survey at Memorial University in St. John's.
He asked some of the professors a number of questions.
One of the questions went this way:
 "What do you do with your money?"
Another question asked:
 "Are you satisfied with the performance of your investments?"
  or "How are your investments doing?"
He later reported that he had received a variety of answers.
To his surprise and to mine there were *some* professors
 who actually did have financial investments.
Then, there was the majority of us
 who had to content ourselves with telling him
  that what doesn't exist, cannot perform,
   with or without satisfaction.
One person had a rather good answer for the questions.
It summed up our situation.
It worked only because she and the investment representative
 were speaking about two different things.
When she was asked about the performance of her investments,
 she replied:
 "I have been investing rather heavily
 in futures lately."
She meant one thing, the education of young people,
 while the investment representative understood her
  to mean something else.
Apparently, in the investment business,
 "investing in futures" is a risky thing to do.

It is the sort of investment in which only those
  who have lots of capital to spare should become involved.
It is for those who have considerable skill
  in predicting the market.
The man conducting the survey was much impressed with her
  answer!
He knew, as most of us didn't,
  that *"investing in futures"* normally meant "short-selling."
He admired anyone who could do it and prosper.
The professor meant something else entirely.
She meant that she has been speculating in the futures
  of young people during the formative years of their lives.
She meant that she had been investing the best years of her life
  in a cause, in a profession, that has always given her
    the greatest personal satisfaction.
It often provides her with hope for the future, as well.
She is a disciple of Jesus Christ.
She is taking her cue from God,
  who is the original high-risk investor in persons.
God has been speculating on the future of the world
  through an investment in persons for as long
    as human life has existed.
God has been speculating
  on the transformation of men, women, and young people
    by a high-risk investment in the lives of other people.
We know the names of some of the persons
  on whom God seemed to risk everything
    from a human point of view.
There are millions of other persons
  about whom we know nothing
    and of whom we have never heard.
One man, known to us by reputation only, was a swindler.
  He had swindled his brother out of his heritage and future,
    the most precious things a person may have.
      Yet, God speculated on Jacob.
Another man wore a crown at one time and played a harp.
  Unhappily, he did other things as well.

He was guilty of murder, adultery, robbery,
    and of scheming to murder.
How far would you have trusted David, the Shepherd King?
Jesus of Nazareth was a speculator, too.
He, too, invested heavily in unlikely stock, in unlikely futures.
Imagine, for example,
    putting the future of a movement in the trust of someone
        who was rough, quick-tempered and too impulsive!
Imagine investing faith, love, and responsibility in a person
    who lied under pressure in order to save his neck?
If you were starting a movement through which to change some
    thing even as local as your neighbourhood,
        it is unlikely you would have chosen Peter.
Yet, Jesus did!
He called this unpromising human material into his service.
He transformed him!
    With him he transformed the lives of other persons as well.
One class of person who has never been popular
    is the Income Tax collector.
In the ancient world such a person was hated and mistrusted,
    with good reason.
One day Jesus approached a tax collector as he sat at his desk,
    with his pen poised and his papers ready.
Within a few moments Matthew found himself out of his office
    and out onto the street in the company of Jesus.
Would you, if you were organizing a movement
    that required integrity and loyalty,
        put your trust in a person who was involved in greed
            and opportunism?
Jesus was an investor in high-risk futures!
You will have other names to add to the ones I have given you.
Hopefully you will add your own name, and mine as well.
This service, and all others like it,
    remind us that God is speculating in futures as much today
        as at any time in the past.
The future of the work of God in the world

        is being invested in your life and in mine.
God is investing the future of the plan of salvation
    in people who come from every part of the community,
        the educated and the uneducated,
            the promising and the indifferent.
God invests in both the likely and the most unlikely people.
    It is a high-risk venture to invest in any one of us.
When we respond to the summons
    to follow Jesus as Saviour and Lord
        there is a corresponding risk on our part, as well.
We need only think back to the people
    whose names were used as illustration of the risk taken by God.
I wonder what his friends and enemies thought
    when they heard that David, the robber king,
        was writing hymns of singular beauty
            in terms of confession and praise to God.
When they gathered for a cup of coffee on the waterfront,
    what did his fellow fishermen say when they learned that Peter
        had left the security of his nets and boat?
All for the insecurity of a future in the service of God,
    after the manner of Jesus of Nazareth?
How did the other people in the taxation office
    view the departure of Matthew from amongst them?
He left behind the possibility of great wealth
    in response to an invitation from One
        who was not even sure of a place to sleep.
Yet, when it was all over,
    or even while they were still in the midst of it,
        no one of these people could claim
            that he had been misled by God.
Or that the implications of the Call had been misunderstood.
Whenever persons invest their lives in the service of God,
    after the manner of Jesus Christ,
        they know in advance that the dividends
            are not necessarily an easy life, a comfortable life,
                or a life of one's own choosing.

According to the scriptures, when a life is committed
   to the cause of Jesus Christ in the world
      it is a high-risk venture.
Yet, despite that, these high risks are being taken every day.
Amongst the followers of Jesus it has always been true
   that there are people taking chances
      of which no honest broker could possibly approve.
There are people of every age
   who are investing the best treasure they have
      in terms of time, money, influence, love, and service,
         in something that promises no visible guarantee of
         return.
There will be a tomorrow for the Christian faith
   because there are big spenders on its behalf today!
The future is filled with promise,
   only because God is able to use ordinary people,
      people of average potential like ourselves, and remake them,
         in order that they may take part with God
            in remaking the world.
A Christian is someone in whom God has speculated.
   A person who, in turn, has invested the resources
      of his/her life in the service of God.
As Christian disciples in the second millennium
   there is no comfortable pulpit or pew.
Nor will there ever be again.
Many of the things we thought were permanent about the Church
   have turned out to be temporary after all.
It is as if many of the old familiar landmarks
   had been moved during the night while we were asleep.
We thought we heard them moving,
   and we tried not to admit it.
Instead, there are only his footprints going on ahead of us.
If we would follow them we must often take uncertain steps,
   moving even in the darkness *some* times,
      running the risk of being misunderstood *most* times.
If we are honest, we are afraid *all* the time
   of where he might lead us in his service.

The only encouragement in all of this, and it is everything,
   is that we will not be asked to *go* or to *do*
      where he has not *gone* or what he has not *done* before us.
      "If anyone will come after me," said Jesus,
      "let that person *first* deny himself,
      then take up the cross and follow me."
          Amen.

Mark 10:17-27
Hebrews 4:12-16
Proverbs 3:13-18

A Man Came Running

In the first three Gospels
    there is a remarkable story about Jesus and a young rich man.
This popular story had one meaning when it was recorded,
    and another meaning entirely in the Early church.
Like so many stories in Mark's Gospel, this one is set
    against a belief in the imminent end of the world.
Mark believed that the world might end this afternoon.
If not this afternoon, certainly by tomorrow or next week.
Or next month or year at the latest.
It is against that background that the demands of Jesus
    are the more easily understood.
If the world is ending within hours, days, or weeks
    what use to hang onto things that will soon pass away?
Things which in the meantime hinder
    the immediate need to come to terms with God.
As time went by in the early years of the Church,
    and in the Church for 2,000 years since then,
        the end did not come as expected in the Gospels.
The story is not now understood as it once was.
No longer is it an appeal to rid ourselves of whatever we own.[1]
In our day it has become an appeal for spiritual honesty.
An appeal to see everything we are, have, or own
    against the background of our commitment to Christ.
It has long since become a story of universal appeal.
Because it is the story of every person,
    at some stage or other of our lives.[2]
It is a story that deals with a question and answer
    fundamental to human existence.

The question is as old as these biblical accounts
— and much older.
It is as fresh as the latest item in tomorrow's newspaper.
The question has always come from people
who suspect there is more to life
than what they are able to learn, earn, or buy.
Nowhere in literature is the issue put as simply,
or in such a profound manner, as it is in the Gospels.
In the Gospel stories, along with the question and answer,
there is a mixture both of sincerity and self-deception.
A mixture, too, of challenge and disappointment
that we recognize at once as genuine to human experience.
According to Mark, Jesus and his disciples were leaving a district
where they had been teaching and healing.
A young man came running up to them.
He was not just any young man,
nor was he acting out a sudden idea or inspiration.
He was a pious, respectable Church-going sort of person,
which was, perhaps, a style of life he had inherited.
He was rather well-to-do,
perhaps living on an inherited income.
He was educated,
and more important than that, he had intelligence.
Possibly a parental characteristic inherited, as well.
Because his financial security was assured
he had time during which to think and ask questions.
He had everything, apparently, that other people wanted!
Yet, there were times, when he knew within him,
that what he didn't have was more important than what he had.
He didn't have possession of much beyond
what he could appreciate through sight, sound, and touch.
Nowhere in the lavish gifts of his earned or inherited living
was there the secret to "eternal life!"
However, to a person of his intelligence and independence,
this great and serious lack in his life
ought not to prove impossible of achievement.

In addition to the *tokens* of the good life,
    which he already possessed,
        he would acquire the *meaning* of life itself.
It was simply a matter of meeting the right teacher or guru!
In that spirit he ran after Jesus.
    "Good Teacher," he began,
    "what must I *do* to inherit eternal life?"
What a refreshing change!
Here at long last is someone asking the fundamental question!
At long last here is someone with no theological axe to grind.
A person with no disease to be healed.
    With no pathetic appeal for financial help.
The person on his knees before Jesus is asking *the* question.
The question now goes to the heart of the human predicament.
Yet, we sense at once that something is wrong.
Somehow things are not as straightforward as they appear.
To begin with, the young man and the reader of the Gospel
    are taken aback by the reply of Jesus to the question.
Jesus questions both the address and the request.
The Church has preserved a surprising dialogue:
    "Why do you call me good?" asked Jesus.
    "No one is good — but God alone."
Apparently, according to the early preacher,
    the young man had mistaken the sort of teacher Jesus was.
He assumed that Jesus would provide easy answers
    to complex human questions.
A person who would offer simple solutions to basic questions.
    "What must I *do* to inherit eternal life."
In other words:
    "Just let me know what to do, and I will do it."
    "More commandments?"
    "Greater charity?"
    "A more intensive study of the Books of Moses?"
    "Please, Teacher, tell me what I must *do*?"
He was mistaken.
Jesus was not a sort of religious Dr. Phil.

"Dear Dr. Phil,
　　I suffer from loneliness. I have always been awkward
　　and diffident with other people. What must I *do*?"
"Dear Dr. Phil,
　　I go to all the office parties, but no one dances with me.
　　How may I become a more attractive person?
　　The other girls seem to have so much fun. What must I *do*?"
In the answers to these questions,
　　there are things the questioner must do.
Maybe to dress provocatively!
　　　Smile a lot!
　　　　　Have your teeth fixed!
There is a genuine concern in these programs to put
　　the disordered pieces of life back together,
　　　　or together for the first time.
Yet, we know it would be asking *too much* of Dr. Phil,
　　or anyone else, to ask for basic human healing!
Just as it is asking *too little* of Jesus to request from him
　　something to *do* in order to receive eternal life.
The meaning of eternal life, the meaning of life itself,
　　is not going to be found in following advice on things to do!
We know that this is a sermon to people in the Early Church.
The young man stands for the Christian community!
　　"No one is good," said Jesus.
　　"God alone is good.
　　Your question has to do with God.
　　Only with God.
　　Therefore, your questions cannot be answered
　　nor your problem solved
　　until you confront the basic issue
　　of your relationship with God!
　　How do you stand with God?"
Then Jesus listed some of the commandments.
He listed only those that have to do with other people.
You know them, said Jesus:
　　"You must not steal.

You must not kill.
You must not commit adultery.
You must not defraud anyone.
And, you must honour your father and mother."
These are the commandments that bring a person to confront
his or her responsibility for other people.
Which is always a matter of taking God seriously.
No more, no less.
What a surprise this is!
What a disappointment!
"Am I to be treated like a child?
Am I to be brought back to kindergarten,
and taught again the A, B, Cs of religious life?"
In his reply to Jesus he dropped the flattering title.
He said simply, in an aggrieved tone:
"Teacher, ever since my Bar-Mitzvah,
I have kept all these commandments."
In other words,
"If keeping these commandments had provided me
with what I am looking for, I would not be here!"
"I have taken God seriously, seriously enough to come here
and declare, in my own way, that I am spiritually bankrupt!"
"I have kept these commandments from my youth up."
By so saying he confessed how imperfectly
he understood the commandments and what they really require.
It is unlikely he had been a thief, a murderer, a cheat,
or neglectful of his parents in any obvious way.
Doubtless, though, he had been angry with his brother.
He may have been jealous of the possessions of other people.
Perhaps he had entertained thoughts about women,
other than his wife.
He had not always told the truth — even to himself!
In one of Albert Stiftler's letters he wrote:
"Every one of us has a tiger-like disposition, and no one knows
what wickedness he might commit when aroused, *if all
restraints were removed*." (emphasis mine)

In the case of this story the young man replied too easily.
He had overlooked too much in his life when he testified
    that he had kept all these commandments of God.
He had totally misunderstood the spirit of the commandments.
It all amounted to a refusal to take God seriously!
We might have expected Jesus to react quickly and angrily.
The reverse was true.
Mark's Gospel preserves a different reaction entirely.
It reads quite simply:
    "And Jesus looking upon him, loved him."[3]
Jesus loved him!
Neither Matthew nor Luke have a record of this reaction.
It is a part of Mark's conviction about God.
It is a part of the Christian experience with Jesus.
The old Catechism reflects the Markan record when it teaches us
    that we are loved by God from the cradle to the grave.
Not simply after we have put our lives in order.
Not after we have kept all the commandments.
Not even after we have done something for others
    simply because it was the right thing to do.
We are loved long before we begin to be who or what we are.
This is an essential reminder to all of us.
We may have forgotten it.
Perhaps we never believed it anyway.
If so, we are unprepared for the next moment
    in the experience of the young man with Jesus.
Against the background of his love for the young man,
    Jesus took the offensive and showed him how costly
        is the gift of eternal life.
The offensive took the form of a simple statement:
    "You lack one thing; go sell what you have,
    and give it to the poor, and you will have treasure
    in heaven and come, follow me."
In other words the decision is yours.
Wholehearted commitment to God
    requires that nothing else is more important than that!

Which one of us is able to commit to that?
  "Your wealth is your problem."
So is anything else that stands between you
  and your relationship with God.
In the heavy silence that followed
    the young man went away sadly in one direction,
      and Jesus went away disappointed in the other.
The doctor and the patient, if you like,
  were separated by the diagnosis and prescription.
Jesus set the standard for eternal life and it was too high.
The young man, the early Christians,
  had more than enough of this world's goods.
Money is by no means the only obstacle in the way
  to finding the quality of life the scriptures call "eternal."
It is only one of many roadblocks that stand between a person
  and his or her ultimate loyalty to God.
The hurdles differ with the person, the culture, and the time.
  Nevertheless, we face them just the same.
Christians of every sort daily face
  the temptation to leave God out of their decision making.
At the end of things,
  even if we achieve every goal we set for ourselves,
    we shall not thereby have lived!
In his novel, *Doctor Zhivago*, the author describes a scene
  in which a firing squad is about to execute a young man
    who has been accused of treason.
Kneeling in the snow, the young man pleads for his life.
  "Forgive me," he said.
  "Comrades, I'm sorry, I won't do it again. Please let me off.
  Don't kill me. *I haven't lived yet.*"
    "*I haven't lived yet.*"
That is the cry that reaches all of us.
If it has not done so yet, it will at some time in our lives.
It is not the length of life that bothers us.
It is the quality of life that matters.
Without meaning it is already too long, however short it is.

Committed to God, it will never be long enough.
All along the way it will be a life transformed,
    and transforming!
A young man came running to Jesus.
    "What must I do to inherit eternal life?" he asked.
    "Come," said Jesus, "and follow me."
        Amen.

---

1. In about 250 A.D. a man called Anthony was born. When he grew up he read the story in Matthew of the rich young ruler. He, too, was young and wealthy. He gave away everything he had. Even this did not satisfy him. He became a hermit and lived in the desert. He was fed by those who came into the desert to see him.

2. MacVicar, Angus, *Capers In My Kirk* (London: Arrow Books Limited, 1987), p. 30, quoted Stewart Mechie, *Great Men And Movements In The History Of The Church*, as follows: "The material side of existence is not necessarily evil; it is only evil when sought first; but in its proper subordination to spiritual purposes it is good. ... This was Christ's philosophy, in direct contradiction to that of hermit monks."

3. Lamar Williamson, *Mark* (Atlanta: John Knox Press, 1985), p. 83. "He expresses no outrage and makes no denunciations. Rather, he feels love for the man who loves his possessions. In love, Jesus calls; and in calling, he makes a radical demand." See also John R. Donahue, S.J. & Daniel J. Harrington, S.J., *The Gospel Of Mark* (Collegeville, Minnesota: Liturgical Press), pp. 302ff.

Mark 11:1-11
Hebrews 12:1-6
Zechariah 9:9-12

Triumphal? Hardly!

The day began with a cry for help from the side of the road.
The cry came from a blind beggar.
His name was Bartimaeus,
    a name that means either Son of Timaeus
        or Son of The Unclean.
As far as we know, the blind beggar
    had never made an appeal to Jesus before that day.
He heard the commotion created by the pilgrims
    on their way up to Jerusalem to celebrate
        an important Jewish festival.
Someone told him:
    "One of the pilgrims is Jesus of Nazareth."
Excited, he called out:
    "Jesus, Son of David, have mercy on me."
This was the first significant incident that took place
    as Jesus and his disciples
        travelled together toward Jerusalem.
He began to cry out for the healing of his blindness.
    "Jesus! Son of David! Have mercy on me!"
The crowds responded:
    "Be quiet. Don't be such a nuisance."
Not to be deterred, he kept calling out:
    "Jesus, Son of David, have mercy on me!"
Jesus stopped. He called the man to him.
Bartimaeus was miraculously healed of his blindness.
Then he followed Jesus and the crowds
    on their way to Jerusalem.
Once again, the disciples misunderstood the healing.

They had been witnesses to the blind receiving their sight
> on other occasions.
To them it was nothing more unusual than they had seen before.
They were mistaken!
In the Gospels, to have one's sight restored
> is also to be given the gift of *spiritual insight*.
Blind Bartimaeus was healed,
> both of his physical and spiritual blindness.
Those whose eyes have been cleared by Jesus,
> who have insight into who Jesus is,
> > will readily understand all that follows.
We have in Bartimaeus an illustration of persistence
> and of genuine faith.[1]
This healing story made such an impression
> through the years that it has even been
> > the subject of beautiful and dramatic poetry.[2]
Once again, this passage from Mark sets the context
> for the Passion narrative about to begin.
Through this story of the blind beggar
> Mark demonstrates to his readers what faith is
> > and what it means to be a disciple of Jesus.
"These elements," wrote one scholar, "follow one another:
persistent pleading, continual shouting when opposed,
cheering up, coming to Jesus, being questioned by him,
having him open one's eyes, and following him on the road."[3]
That is also the sequence of our own coming to faith in Jesus
> as the Lord of our lives.
The healing of Bartimaeus' sight was the first incident
> in the journey of Jesus and his disciples toward Jerusalem.
There follows an account of Jesus nearing the Holy City.
It is a story we know well.
> It is a story we know as The Triumphal Entry.
Was it really Triumphal? If not, what was it?
Was it not perhaps *anything but Triumphal*?
Was it perhaps more a dramatic and symbolic action
> on the part of Jesus?

A demonstration of the sort the Old Testament prophets
    used to such effectiveness in their day?[4]
These actions, these demonstrations, are also parables.
They are parables acted out in public.
They are demonstrations with a purpose.
    They make people think and ask questions.
Not just while they are being acted out in public,
    but productive of thought and curiosity for years afterward.
The entry of Jesus from the suburbs to the centre of the Holy City,
    was a trip of two miles.
As Mark records it, it was one of the most moving
    and mysterious events in the life of Jesus.
It was a mysterious event mainly because it seems
    so out of character for Jesus to take part
        in any sort of noisy demonstration.
It was a moving event if for no other reason than the attempt
    it represents to say something in action
        that had been ignored in words.
Sometimes it is necessary for a teacher to do something dramatic,
    to do something desperate, in order to teach a lesson
        or illustrate a truth.
It was a teaching technique with a long history in Jesus' people,
    a technique with which he would have been familiar.
Quite apart from the Old Testament examples,
    we may quite properly cite those twentieth century
        ones of Mahatma Gandhi and Martin Luther King, Jr.[5]
These men gave their lives for a cause
    to which they were completely committed.
They demonstrated, they acted out in the causes of freedom
    and equality of race and class.
Good drama is always more effective than a talk or a sermon.
If done well it will use colour and movement.
In the case of Jesus as a pilgrim on that day,
    there were the sounds of many feet on the hard road
        and the clip-clop of the donkey as it walked along.
Drama is most often accompanied by a variety of sound.

In the case of Jesus' pilgrimage into Jerusalem,
    there was the noise of conversation amongst the pilgrims.
There were the shouts that accompany such events.
Drama is effective in the communication of emotions,
    or feelings, whether serious or light.
A mood is created, an atmosphere is communicated.
Mark records this particular parable,
    Jesus is riding a donkey in the middle of the crowd.
There are fellow pilgrims walking both before and after him.
The donkey on which Jesus rode was a symbol
    both of Royalty and of Peace.
Jesus carried neither sword nor any trophies.
He led no prisoners nor were his hands raw with killing.
Those who followed him were fellow pilgrims, not prisoners.
Those who went before him and those who followed
    shouted:
        "The Kingdom of Our Father David that is coming."
They also sang the words of Psalms 118 and 119:
    "Hosanna To The Son of David."
Words which mean:
    "Save us, we beseech Thee O Lord."[6]
Branches, or straw, as the text has it,
    and cloaks were said to have been laid down
        before Jesus as he went on his way.[7]
He was surrounded by fellow pilgrims,
    symbolic of their devotion to God.
He might as well have been accompanied by bodyguards.
No one noticed who or what he was.
He had tears in his eyes,
    but he might as well have sneered in contempt.
No one noticed.
He had come to announce the reign of God
    in the hearts of the people of God.
His supporters, meanwhile, strained to hear him
    call for a bloody revolution.
He had entered his city, their city,

to proclaim the peace that only God can give.
His fellow demonstrators were eager to fight
 and if need be to die for freedom from an occupation army.
He saw our enemies as primarily those of the mind and spirit.
His fellow countrymen saw them as wearing Roman army
 uniforms.
The demonstration was intended to point up the contrast
between the power of the world and the power of the Spirit of God.
Troops and weapons can *enforce* peace and order.
They do not *create* peaceful people.
The demonstration on that day went beyond his control.
It achieved nothing of what he had intended it to do.
He had been misunderstood once again.
He allowed the superficial enthusiasm of the journey to die
 and the people to disperse.
At the end of the day we are left with a haunting picture.
A picture of a lonely figure looking around the Temple,
 as any tourist might do.
Finally, after every other demonstration had failed,
 he demonstrated again, on Friday morning at 9 o'clock,
  when he staked his life on the love of God.
   Amen.

---

1. Eduard Schweizer, *The Good News According To Mark*, trans. by Donald H. Madvig (Atlanta: John Knox Press, 1970), p. 227. "Mark demonstrates to his readers what faith is and what it means to be a disciple of Jesus. These elements follow one another: persistent pleading, continual shouting when opposed, cheering up, coming to Jesus, being questioned by him, having him open one's eyes, and following him on the road. When a man's eyes have been opened by a divine miracle, he can see what is happening in Jesus and can 'follow Jesus on the road.'"

2. David Lyle Jeffrey, Editor, *A Dictionary Of Biblical Tradition In English Literature* (Grand Rapids, Michigan: Wm. B. Eerdmans Publishing Company, 1992), pp. 76-77. "The most notable poem on the subject in English is Longfellow's 'Blind Bartimaeus,' actually a macaronic Greek/English poem which casts the event as a dramatic paradigm for the condition of all people who would be healed of spiritual blindness. Both John Newton (1179) and, later in the nineteenth century, George Macdonald also wrote poems on the subject."

3. Eduard Schweizer, *Op Cit.*, p. 225.
   E.P. Blair, *The Interpreter's Dictionary Of The Bible*. Vol. A-D. (Tennessee: Abingdon Press, 1962), p. 361.

4. See Isaiah 20:1-6; Jeremiah 13:1-11; 28:1-17; 31:1-5; Ezekiel 2:1-33; and Hosea 20:1; 2:1.

5. John R. Donahue, S.J., & Daniel Harrington, S.J., *The Gospel Of Mark* (Collegeville, Minnesota: The Liturgical Press, 2002), p. 323. "Mark's account of Jesus' entry into Jerusalem is best understood as a symbolic action or prophetic demonstration, analogous to the public actions used so effectively by OT prophets and in the twentieth century by Mahatma Gandhi and Martin Luther King, Jr."
   The names of other men and women throughout history may be added to that list.

6. Samuel Tobias Lachs, *A Rabbinic Commentary On The New Testament: The Gospels Of Matthew, Mark, And Luke* (Hoboken, New Jersey: KTAV Publishing House, Inc., 1987), pp. 344-345.

7. Lachs, *Op Cit.*, "Reminiscent of 2 Kings 9:13, p. 344, 'Then in haste every man of them took his garment and put it under him on the bare steps, and they proclaimed Jehu is King.'"
   "Of Naqdimon B. Gorion it is related that when he went from his house to the House of Study they would spread out woollen garments under him. Mention is made of spreading carpeting from homes to the graves of Davidic kings; and of spreading a carpet for the high priest from his house to the Temple." *Ibid.*

Mark 12:1-11
Ezekiel 34

Noises In The Vineyard

One of the increasingly familiar features of the North American
    landscape is the presence of vineyards.
Especially is this true in Canada
    from Nova Scotia to British Columbia.
In America we think at once of the Napa Valley in California,
    as only one of many examples.
These vineyards make a significant contribution
    to the local and national economy.
As a result, the owners are important people.
However, the vineyard is not as important in either country
    as it was in the eastern world in the decades
        before and after the lifetime of Jesus.
In his country, Jesus and his fellow countrymen
    took the vineyard for granted.
It was there, as in North America,
    a necessary part of the national and domestic landscape.
However, 2,000 years ago, the vineyard was rarely, if ever,
    owned by a local person.
Many of the men who owned the vineyards in Palestine
    lived so far away they rarely visited their investment.
It was a situation not that unlike the investment in Canada
    of capital from business people in the United Kingdom,
        the United States, the various Arab countries, and Japan.
As in Canada, it was often true in Palestine that a local manager
    and a staff of workers looked after the foreign owned business
        on some sort of profit sharing basis.
At the end of each harvest,
    when the grapes had been made into wine,
        the owner sent a representative to collect
            up to forty percent of the net profit.

The remainder was divided between the manager and the tenants.
There were instances in which the owner,
    unlike the situation in Canada, was cheated
        of his proper share in the profits.
Quite apart from the biblical account of this situation,
    there are other stories of local staff taking matters
        into their own hands and mistreating the visiting accountant.
Because the importance of a vineyard was recognized by everyone,
    it could be used as a parable of the People of God.
One of the great figures to use the vineyard as a parable
    of the relationship between God and the People of God was Isaiah.
Thereafter, the vineyard became a common expression
    for the Reign of God.
Many years after it had been used by Isaiah,[1]
    the parable of the vineyard was taken up by Jesus,
        who expanded it and applied it once again to the People
            of God.
Jesus used the parable to emphasize the difference between
    the behaviour God expects from the People of God
        and what behaviour, if any, God receives from them.
Since the difference between the two is a profound one,
    the People of God are in a serious position.
They find themselves in a situation
    where judgment has already begun.
It is the inevitable effect of their accumulated misbehaviour.
The folk to whom Jesus spoke were ready to agree with him
    on the discrepancy between what God expected and received.
They were *not* ready to believe that because of it,
    certain consequences would befall them.
In an ideal vineyard, the concern of the tenants ought to be
    a local expression of the Reign of God in the world.
They are trustees of the vineyard.
They have been given temporary custody of something
    that does not, nor ever will, belong to them.
They have been given opportunities and privileges
for the sole purpose of serving the world in the name of God.

They have money and position to be used for the relief of the world
 as if these were a towel and a basin of water.
They see themselves as disciples of the Man from Nazareth,
 commissioned by him to express the love of God
  with and for the People of God.
The messengers of God come to the Church
 as they came to the People of God in the time of Jesus.
They come to us, not as accountants, but as opportunities.
Wherever there are Christians in any part of the world,
 there are also the messengers of God.
These messengers vary in number and in nature but still they come
 as they have done for more than twenty centuries.
When they come they expect no more than an authentic expression
 of Christian discipleship.
Nothing more is expected of us than behaviour
 consistent with our convictions.
As a whole the People of God have not left a record
 that should surprise us with joy.
Yet, always there have been, and are, individuals
 so convinced of their discipleship that the Church
  has been spared the judgment hanging over it.
In what form do you think the messengers of God
 are visiting the Church in 2006?
Where do you sense opportunities for discipleship
 in our present secular society?
Perhaps it is not as easy for other people to recognize
 an opportunity in which Christians ought to act,
  as it is for those of us who are.
One of the first lessons a child of Christian parents
 is taught concerns the love of God.
A little later the child is taught that God expects us
 to love one another as we are loved by God.
In fact, we understand the New Testament to say that unless
 we love one another, we are unable to be loved by God.
It is the main commandment of discipleship that we love our
 neighbour as we do ourselves.

The commandment does not say that we may love everyone
> except those who do not speak as we do, worship as we do,
>> or live as we do.

We are to love one another,
> not simply for the cultural benefits from so doing.

Rather, we are to love one another
> because we are all equally the children of God.

In this period of national and international uneasiness,
> the disciples of Jesus, of whatever tongue or denomination,
>> might be expected to put into practice the oneness of
>> humanity under the God that we preach.

There is room for diversity
> and no room for hatred of race, colour, or creed.

We know better than to expect politicians of any stripe
> in any country to take a stand against military aggression
>> as it affects the weakest members of the children of God.

As Christians, we know that God does expect the People of God
> to believe that war and hate propaganda are wrong.

That racial discrimination is wrong.

That no nation may, with impunity, ruin the reputation
> of another one by a skillful manipulation of the mass media.

The recent aggression by Hezbollah in Lebanon
> prompts us to shout as loudly as is possible:
>> "Thus says the Lord: You shall not in my name (or any other)
>> take the lives of my children."

The accountant came to the vineyard because it belongs to God.

He looked to the tenants for a full measure of justice
> and he overheard a permission to massacre.

In the story of the vineyard there is no record
> in Mark's Gospel what if anything the greedy tenants did
>> to those tenants who disagreed with the majority.

Perhaps they were not allowed to leave the vineyard alive.

As the parable of the vineyard is applied to the Church,
> it must be said that some tenants in the vineyard find it
>> necessary to leave it.

In the *London Telegraph* is a report of the young people

who, early in their theological education and spiritual
formation, terminate their training for the ministry
within the Church of England.
There are others who begin well and shortly afterward leave.
What happens, then, when God sends an opportunity for service?
There happens precisely what we have come to expect
would happen under the circumstances.
The tenants are busy perpetuating ancient division
and regurgitating ancient statements of faith.
They are busy with offerings to the great god called "Status Quo."
There is no time for opportunities of service,
especially if these should come from God.
Ah, now then, did someone say the vineyard belongs to God?
Is the Church really the Church of God and not the private preserve
of those persons who control it?[2]
Yes, it is the Church of God.
It is the place where Christ has chosen to dwell.
The Man from Nazareth said so!
"What," he asked, "will the owner of the vineyard do?
He will come and destroy the tenants, and give the vineyard
to others."
The vineyard is the Kingdom of God and the tenants
are the People of God. The members of the Church!
The messengers are the opportunities of service
that come to the disciples.
If the messengers are turned away indefinitely,
the discipleship will be destroyed.
Do you hear them?
The noises in the vineyard, I mean? I hear them.
I pray to God they are the noises of those
who do the will of God among the People of God.
Amen.

1. Lamar Williamson, *Mark* (Atlanta: John Knox Press, 1983), pp. 215f, for a full discussion of the contrast between use of the vineyard imagery in Isaiah and the allegory of it in Mark.

2. *Ibid*, p. 216. "Be careful lest in clamoring for your place in the vineyard you reject the Son whose way is service and a cross. The warning originally addressed to arrogant Jewish leaders applies equally to arrogant Christian leaders today."

Mark 12:13-17
Romans 13:1-7

Sharing The Burden

Within recent months the Canadian provincial ministers
 of both Health and Finance met in Ottawa.
They went, as usual, to negotiate
 for a larger piece of the federal budget.
Despite their forceful arguments in support of their demands,
 despite their bursts of outrage about arrogance in Ottawa, the
  Federal Finance Minister refused to share a penny with
   them.
Canadians are growing accustomed to watching
 these annual tug-of-war matches in Ottawa.
We are so used to hearing the same arguments from both sides
 that many of us are no longer able to decide the rightness
  of either side.
The imposition of a tax on its people is a basic source
 of government income.
The citizens rarely enjoy it.
At least once a year they make a determined effort
 to avoid as much of it as possible.
The imposition of a tax on its citizens is one
 of the oldest forms of financing projects by the State
  for its citizens.
It was Poll Tax time again when
 some tax evasion experts came to Jesus.[1]
The men who came to Jesus knew as well as he did
 how much this tax, and all taxation, was hated.
  "What about the taxation?" they asked him.
  "Should we pay the Poll Tax or not?"
  "Do you think it is legal for the government
  to hit everyone with the same figure?"

It was an attempt on their part to be clever.
If Jesus agreed with the tax,
>   they intended to turn the people against him.

If he disagreed with it, they intended to have him
>   arrested for treason.
>   >   "Who has a quarter?" Jesus asked.
>   >   "Whose picture is on the other side?"
>   >   "Is this *your* picture?"
>   >   "Is it perhaps the picture of your *father*?"
>   >   "No," they replied, "It is the picture of the Ruler.
>   >   On the other side is written his name."
>   >   "Then," said Jesus, "The money belongs to him,
>   >   >   does it not?²
>   >   >   Give him what you owe him.
>   >   >   Remember, though, that there is an area of life which
>   >   >   belongs to God.
>   >   >   That part of life is more important than the Poll Tax."

Or, as it is in the biblical text:
>   "Give to Caesar the things that are his,
>   and to God the things that belong to God."

A simple answer to the question about paying taxes.
It has been the basis for the Christian attitude
>   toward the State ever since.

Jesus taught that the State has certain basic rights.
There is an area of life in which the State exercises
>   legitimate control.

In the exercise of that control
>   it may correctly expect the support of its people.

The Statement of Faith of the Reformed Churches has in it:
>   "The State is ordained by God for the well-being of man."

In other words, it is as much commissioned by God
>   to do its work as the Church is commissioned by God
>   >   to extend the Reign of God over the lives of men,
>   >   women, and children.

In both Church and State, God works through sinful people.
Let no one suppose that the sinners in one area are worse
>   than their brothers and sisters in the other!

The Church and State have in common
    both fallible leadership and membership.
The source of their common authority lies
    outside themselves entirely.
There is no indication in Scripture or tradition
to indicate that God regards either the Church or the State
as superior to the other in the exercise of the will of God
in the world.
Each one has a particular function,
    for which it is peculiarly fitted to perform.
For instance, the Reformed Churches teach that
    the State is specially commissioned by God
        to serve in the administration of justice.
Insofar as an injustice is done to anyone,
    the State is held accountable to God.
The State is responsible to God for the control
    of our economic lives so that no one is destitute.
It is duty bound to concern itself
    with the obvious physical needs of its citizens.
In all things, the State is reminded that it exists
    for the benefit of those on whose behalf it governs.
It does not exist, as sometimes seems, for the benefit of itself.
Day to day living would spiral down into chaos
    without the laws that govern living.
The spirit of the age, especially with the immigration
of many who do not share our values or procedures,
is to rebel against all regulations, whether
they are worthy or unworthy.
Many would substitute for our system of justice
    a system of their own.
There are certain laws necessary before people
    can live together in a community of persons.
Unless those laws command the respect and obedience of all of us,
    the breakdown of "life-in-community" is imminent.
The Church teaches a high doctrine of the State.
It holds high expectations of its role in life

because it recognizes the source of State authority
    as residing in God.
We may and do grumble about our taxes.
Yet, without them very few people are able to provide
    for themselves the things we take for granted
    as necessary for living.
We are unhappy about the costs of civic administration.
Despite that, it brings with it protection and opportunities
    we should otherwise be without.
The arrangements made by the State for the retirement of those
    whose working days are over are far from perfect.
Yet, without them many people would be unhappier
    and worse off than they are.
Civil obedience is an obligation
    when the demands of the State are moral.
When they are immoral, when they clash with the conscience of
Christians, we are under an equal obligation to disobey them.
There are certain areas of life over which
    Caesar has no legitimate control.
When Caesar begins to take the place of God
    in the determination of human destiny, he must be rebuked.
When the State is corrupt
    it may be a life threatening matter to rebuke it.
The history of warfare is replete with the names of those
    who tried and who died for their attempts to do it.
Our first duty as Christians is to obey God
    and then willingly to accept the consequences.
It is a pathetic sort of person who is willing to accept
all the benefits provided by the State
and then refuse to accept some responsibility for them.
There are times when Christians owe it to God and their fellow
citizens to be as much involved in the political life of their
country as they ought to be in the Church.
The responsibilities of citizenship,
    like the responsibilities of Church membership,
        involve us in a process of making decisions and taking
        action.

Unless people are living under a totalitarian regime,
    they have a share in the decisions that are made.
The Christian disciple is a loyal citizen.
However, there have been and are groups of Christians
    who avoid political life for fear of contamination.
That is surely naive.
In both Church and State we are working with people first,
    policies and programs afterward.
The coin that was shown to Jesus
    bore the image of the Ruler at the time.
The coin in your pocket bears the image of the Sovereign.
Therefore, *legally*, it belongs to her.
The Christian conviction is that a person bears the image of God.
Therefore, we belong to God.
When the State remains within its appointed boundaries
    and makes legitimate demands, we owe it our loyalty
        and service.
We share in the burden of responsibility
    for the decisions that affect us.
However, the State as well as its people belong to God.
It follows that if at any time the claims of the State
    conflict with those of God, loyalty to God comes first.
It is as true today as it has been for centuries
    that, under normal circumstances, our Christian faith
        should make us better citizens than anyone else.
It is as a part of our discipleship that we present ourselves
    willing to share the burdens for the benefits we receive.
        Amen.

1. C.E.B. Cranfield, *The Gospel According To Mark* (Cambridge: Cambridge University Press, rep. 11 times, latest in 2000), p. 369. "In any case it is likely that it was either the Sanhedrin as such or else some members of it who sent the questioners."

   For a slightly different understanding of the questioners, see Lamar Williamson, Jr., *Mark* (Atlanta: John Knox Press, 1983), pp. 218f.

2. *Ibid*. p. 372.
   Interesting is the discussion of this pericope in John R. Donahue, S.J. and Daniel J. Harrington, S.J., *The Gospel Of Mark* (Collegeville, Minnesota: The Liturgical Press, 2002), pp. 345-348.

Mark 12:41-44
Hebrews 10:11-18
Daniel 12:1-4

Who Gives What To The Budget?

Following a series of debates with some tough-minded people,
    Jesus sat down facing a row of wickets in a Church bank.
These were wickets of the old-fashioned bank variety,
    and all of them were prepared to receive offerings.
Above each wicket was a notice,
    stating the cause for which the offerings were received.
Taken all together, these notices represented every concern
    of religious people:
        from repairs to the temple roof,
            to the relief of the poor and much, much more.
The people came up to the wickets,
    announced the amount of their offerings,
        and then dropped them into the appropriate slot.
There was a constant noise as the money fell
    into large metal containers.
The sounds coming to the ears of Jesus
    were not unlike those of the old-fashioned
        cash registers in a department store.
Many of you are much too young to have known of them.
At first he paid no attention to what was going on around him.
He sat immobile with his head in his hands.
His mind was a confusion of ideas.
His body was exhausted.
It was when he began to feel more like himself
    that he watched the proceedings with some interest.
While he watched,
    a wealthy merchant came up to a counter.

He said clearly: $500.00.
Having said that, he put his money into the container.
After he left, two well-to-do landlords came into the bank.
Each man put $75.00 into the offering,
    at the same time announcing the amount in a clear voice.
These were religious people, doing business with God.
They were making their offerings on this day
    as they had been taught to do from childhood.
There were women in the bank, as well.
Some of them were well dressed in apparel that was as
    exclusive in design as it was in its material.
The majority were more modestly attired.
They walked up the wickets
    and quietly declared their offerings.
Jesus did not always hear what they said.
He was thinking about these people and their gifts
    for the Temple and the work of God,
        when Poverty walked into the hall.
In this instance Poverty was a woman, a widow
    who lived on the edge of starvation from one day to the next.
Watching her come into the room, Jesus might have assumed
    she was weary and looking for a place to rest.
The woman was preoccupied with other thoughts.
She watched anxiously for an opportunity and then,
    going to the counter, she announced clearly: "Two Pennies."
Having dropped them into one of the great metal chests,
    she was gone.
For the first time that afternoon Jesus was so excited
    he called out for the disciples.
When he had gathered them round him,
    they held the first discussion in the Church
        about the offerings people make to God.
What the disciples were taught that day has been the basis
    ever since for our attitude toward the offering.
There are several things in this discussion
    that stand out from the rest.

The Church must know, taught Jesus,
   how to measure the value of an offering to God.
The Church needs to recognize the spirit
   in which such an offering is made.
When the Temple officers counted the offerings that evening,
   they were not concerned with the individuals who made them.
Nor with their attitudes toward giving.
Their concern was the total amount!
In their reckoning, the gift of $500.00
   from the wealthy merchant would go almost 7 times as far
      as the donation from one of the landlords.
Either of those gifts would reduce to nothing
   the value of the amount from the poor widow.
Her offering might buy oil for the hinges of a door,
   but nothing more.
Unhappily, the figures in a ledger,
   unlike the words in a love letter, tell us nothing
      of the person who put them there.
The disciples then realized that the scale of values
   in the reign of God is a vastly different one from the one
      the world uses.
Until he had pointed it out to them
   they had not imagined that the gift of the widow
      was the largest transaction of the day.
The amount of the offering, taught Jesus,
   is never of a fixed value.
      It is always a relative thing.
The person of fortune, for example, who gives $500.00 each week
   may be giving much less than the girl or boy who,
      from a paper route, gives fifty cents per week.
The gift is measured *not* by what is given,
   but by what is left over!
The generosity of those who give freely
   is everywhere commended in scripture.
The value depends on *how much* is left untouched.

The value of a small offering is very high indeed,
> when it comes from a person who has little left
>> for himself or herself.

It is the *spirit* of the woman's offering we are to emulate
> not the amount.

The lesson for discipleship in the life of the widow
> ought to be on the Christian conscience.

It is simply that our Lord measures our offering
> by the amount we have left untouched.

The significant gift is the one that costs the giver the most.
> Whether the gift comes from a person of modest means
>> or of great wealth.

The Christian religion recognizes that what we do with our time
> and money is a good expression of our discipleship.

It recognizes, too, that just as revealing
> as the amount of time and money we return to God
>> is the spirit in which it is done.

For 400 years the Churches in our tradition
> throughout the world faithfully stressed the material
>> opportunities and responsibilities of worship.

So much was this true that its members throughout the world
> were identified with generosity in giving to the work
>> and worship of the Church.

You may remember the old definition of the ideal Church?

It was "one that Sang like Methodists, Prayed like Anglicans,
> and Gave like Presbyterians!"

In the last 25 years we have lost that reputation.

The average offerings today are smaller, in proportion
> to our affluence, than they were during the days of the
>> depression in the 1930s.

We believe, surely, that we belong to God,
> that we are ambassadors of God and to do the will of God.

Basic to our belief is that we do not exist for ourselves!

The scriptures teach us more about the opportunities
> for discipleship, in terms of income and ability,
>> than they do about sin, prayer, preaching, or God.

What, in your mind, is the clearest sign that Christianity

is failing to make a positive impression on its followers
    in the modern world?
Some people answer that question in terms of the empty pews
    in far too many of our churches across Canada.
There are others who see our inability to come together
    as one great world Church as a sign that Christianity
        is dead — even within the discipleship.
Other thoughtful people see our inability as Christians,
    to be peace makers in the many trouble-spots of the world.
All of these are significant pointers of the state
    of our spiritual health or sickness.
However, it is whenever I hear offerings being coaxed
out of Christian people for the cause of the Church of Christ
that failure stares me in the face.
To coax, blackmail, or threaten Christians to give to God
    is surely *the* sign of decadence and approaching death.
The account in Mark of Jesus and the offering
    is one that Christians have always loved.
It taught the poor that no gift is too small.
It taught the more affluent that their gifts,
    of whatever size, are worthy of them and of God,
        — in terms of what is left untouched.
            Not by the amount given.
It teaches us that in whatever state we are, the gift
    that counts for much is the one that costs us much.[1]
The story of Jesus and the offering is a reminder
    that you and I cannot be lectured into giving what
        what we ought to give.
No one need tell us that the first mark of discipleship
    is to give with happiness and generosity.
This much we already know! This is what we believe!
The person who can hear and understand this story from Mark
    will be moved to an examination of his or her return
        to God and the Church of God.
Those who are not moved to self-examination by the story
    have become insensitive to one of the basic requirements of

Christian discipleship.
Amen.

---

1. Eduard Schweizer, *The Good News According To Mark*, Trans. Donald H. Madvig (Atlanta: John Knox Press, 1970), pp. 259ff. "Thus this brief story exalts that quiet, matter-of-course and total giving which does not make a fuss about the deed. Letting go of himself and every security the person commits himself completely to God's mercy. Accordingly, it makes a good conclusion to Jesus' public ministry."

Mark 13:32-37
1 Corinthians 1:3-9
Isaiah 63:16—64:4

The End!

On Friday and Saturday evenings, on a very busy corner,
  in downtown Chilliwack, a man walks back and forth.
He carries a sign.
It reads and he shouts:
  "The End is Near! The Lord Is Coming Soon!"
Generally, people ignore him.
They simply walk past him and say nothing.
It may come as a surprise that the 13th chapter of Mark
  says the same thing as the man on the street corner.
There are big words associated with the reading from Mark.
Words like *eschatology* and *apocalyptic*.
In its basic meaning, "eschatology"
  refers to matters concerning the *end* of the world.
The whole of chapter 13 in Mark
  is concerned with the *end* of time.
Mark has put some strange sounding words
  in the mouth of Jesus.
For instance, verse 30 in chapter 13 reads:
  "Truly, I say to you this generation will not pass away before
  all these things take place. Heaven and earth will pass away,
  but my words will not pass away."
Comments concerning the End of the world,
  the End of all things, are matters of eschatology.
The details of what will happen as the end of Time approaches
  are matters included in "apocalyptic" literature.
For example, verses 14 onward read:
  "But when you see the desolating sacrilege set up where it ought
  not to be (let the reader understand), then let those who are
  in Judea flee to the mountain."

A little farther, the writer goes on:
    "Pray that it may not happen in winter.
    For in those days there will be such tribulation
    as has not been from the beginning of creation which God
    created until now, and never will be."
All of chapter 13 in Mark is called The Little Apocalypse.
The Great Apocalypse is the Book of Revelation.
Chapter 13, then, concerns the *end* of time
    and of what happens leading up to it.
The stress is on the necessity of preparation
    for something that is inevitable.
At one time or other you had to write an examination of some sort.
You may be a person who enjoys or who enjoyed examinations.
Many of us would rather neither write nor mark them,
    if we had a choice in the matter.
Whether the examination is enjoyable or unpleasant there is,
    under normal circumstances, advance notice of it.
Students need time sufficient to make preparation for it.
That would be a matter of eschatology.
Some professors or teachers make it a policy to spring
    an examination on students without any warning.
In such a class the students face examinations or tests
    according to a pattern or whim known only to the instructor.
The best students in these classes keep their work up-to-date,
    just in case a test might be given when it is least expected.
Those who are well prepared have no problems.
Those who are unprepared had nothing but problems.
Anyone who has travelled by air has watched the routine
    demonstration on the use of oxygen masks.
The demonstration is so routine that many people pay little
    or no attention to it.
On a flight some years ago, a seasoned traveller continued to read the morning paper while the use of the mask was being demonstrated and explained.
When the demonstration was finished
    he turned to the person in the seat next to him.

He said:
   "I wonder when those things were last used.
   Not ever, I suspect."
His companion replied:
   "We used them yesterday, on a flight out of New York."
   "Really?" responded the first man.
   "What did she say again?"
A little later he reached, ever so casually, for the information
card in the seat packet and began to read it in a casual manner.
The man did not want to appear anxious.
However, he was unable to resist a bit of preparation,
   just in case.
There is no substitute for preparation in anticipation
   either of the expected or the unexpected.
The greater part of our lives is spent doing ordinary things
   and in making routine preparation for day-to-day living.
This is as it has to be.
From time to time the routine and the repetition
   become hypnotic in their total effect on us.
The repetition and the routine induce a false sense of security.
They presume that personal and community history
   are like a river down which we move in slow and steady progress.
They presume there are no hidden rocks in the stream.
No sudden waterfall or boiling whirlpool.
They presume, too, that personal and communal history
   are without a purpose.
Other than to take part in the ride down the river.
The routine preparation we make for life and living
   avoids the possibility of any significant meaning
      in our existence.
A line or two on a gravestone
   do not make an adequate commentary on our lives.
Sometime during our lifetime,
   somewhere between the announcement of our birth
      and the notice of our death,
         there ought to have begun a conversation
           between us and God.

The steady movement of a guided boat down a stream is not an adequate representation of the way in which individuals and communities live.
It is "fatal" for a person to be heedless
    of purpose or destiny in life.
It is just as "fatal" for a person to become totally absorbed
    in what appears to be the even tenor of the routine.
Perhaps "fatal" seems to you too strong a word
    to use in this context.
Not really.
It is not too strong a word to use were we thinking only
    of people who fail to prepare for the regular routine of life.
According to the Mark, Jesus thought it a good word and idea
    to apply to those who are heedless of the signs around them
        that there is more to life than length of days.
Not that there is something wrong with length of days,
    but it does not explain the purpose of life.
It does not justify our existence.
When or where should a person begin to do serious business
    and to take part in a conversation with God?
Well, when did you begin your relationship with God?
It may have been, as with many of us, in our homes
    and the Christian convictions of our parents.
When we are little we are taught to pray in simple language.
We are taught to repeat a blessing at mealtime.
It is quite like the increasing responsibility of a person
    from childhood to becoming an adult in other ways.
For example, when a person is young he or she
    is given a little pocket money.
The child is allowed to buy something at a store.
That is the beginning of the child's commercial life.
By the time a person is a teenager,
    the spending habits are considerably increased.
A larger allowance with some responsibilities for it.
Many earn their own money in their early teen years.
When the child becomes an adult, business affairs
    are conducted with maturity and responsibility.

When a child begins to communicate with a parent,
communication is done through signs and then simple words.
Long before there is conversation, there is communication.
When the teenage years arrive,
    those who know and love them may wonder
        whether this is the same person
            who once had no speech at all!
The young person is then, ideally,
    a responsible partner in any conversation.
When one is an adult, the conversation will, hopefully,
    correspond to the level of one's maturity,
        experience, and education.
According to Mark, Jesus expected
    that the same would be true of his disciples.
That their growth in faith would be reflected
    in their conversations with God.
The children of Christian parents are taught
    that life has a deeper meaning than their standing in society
        or the size of their bank accounts.
As with a child beginning to do business with others
    or to communicate with them,
        what begins in simple fashion in one's awareness of God
            should mature and develop as we mature and develop
                in every other way.
The belief that life has a meaning beyond our shaping of it
    and a purpose that lies beyond anything or anyone we may
        manipulate, begins with the simplest conversations
            of a child with God.
The questions of a little child about God are every bit as
    important as are his or her prayers.
The questions are forms of a conversation with God.
The level of our responsibility in our personal relationship
    with God is not an obscure or a mysterious matter at all.
It is quite obvious to anyone of spiritual perception
    with whom we may associate.
The biographer of Dr. William Morris includes
    an interesting comment by that brilliant person.

It goes like this:
> "I used really to despair once because I thought
> what the idiots of our day call 'progress' would go on
> perfecting itself: happily, I know that all this
> will have a sudden check — sudden in appearance that is."

This is eschatological language!
Not everyone believes that what is called "progress"
    will one day come to an end.
There is much that we hope will not come to an end.
Either suddenly or what will appear to be a sudden event.
Not everyone believes that quite apart from the New Age
    in which we are living because of the life, death,
        and resurrection of Jesus, one day the scroll of history
        will be completely unrolled, run out!
According to Mark, Jesus believed it.
So did many of his disciples then and so do many now.
THE END, two words full of meaning for everyone and everything.
They appear at the end of empires and civilizations,
    of institutional usefulness and of professional service.
They are written after the final chapter
    of both personal and communal life.
These are inevitable words!
They represent an unavoidable event!
Only God knows when it will happen, and where and how.
It is our responsibility to be prepared for it, all of the time.
THE END is like the examination set
    at the discretion of the lecturer.
The students who hoped to pass it had to do their
    homework all the time.
It is like travelling by air and meeting a crisis without warning.
The passengers who are prepared are the ones
    with the best chances of survival.
They have read the survival hints.
They have listened to the instructions of the flight attendants.
During the moment when you are faced with a situation in which
you have to deal with the reality of God in your life, the best

preparation will have been a lifetime of intimate conversation with God.
A lifetime of faithful service to God, through Jesus Christ our Lord, who is both the Beginning and the End of all things.
Amen.

Mark 14:12-26
Phillipians 2:5-11
Isaiah 45:21-25

The Divine Drama

The many divisions in the institutional Church perpetuate
    many unfortunate situations.
For example, there are branches of the Holy Catholic Church
    which continue to refuse participation in the Sacrament
        of Holy Communion to non-members.
In general, however, there are preserved certain unmistakable
    marks in the Church as the Body of Christ.
Those of us in the Reformed tradition have cause to be grateful
    that our forefathers retained so many of them.
At the time of the Reformation brave men restated the theology
    of the sacraments.
It fell to even bolder men to give this restatement
    an expression in word and action.
To these people we trace the forms we use today.
We claim that whenever the sacraments
    are properly celebrated in the Church,
        we are obedient to the practice of the Early Church
            in Jerusalem.
However, as a cautionary note,
    if we are obedient to the Apostolic Church in most of the
        essentials surrounding Holy Communion,
        we confess to disobedience in one of them.
Today, no responsible minister or Church member claims,
    for example, to trace our infrequency of the celebration
        to the New Testament or to the Apostolic Church.
We cannot read the Book of Acts without concluding
    that *whenever* Christians met for worship, they remembered
        the Passion of Christ and celebrated his Presence.

At the same time, we know that if the Reformed Church
	has been neglectful in this way,
		it has not been unmindful in many other ways.
She has preserved for us a magnificent expression
	of the most wonderful thing we do in the Church.
When we gather for a celebration of Holy Communion,
	there are signs or there is symbolism in what is seen
		and heard and done in the celebration of Holy Communion.
To say nothing of the *reality* to which the symbolism points us.[1]
Following the conclusion of Vatican 2, members of the Reformed
	tradition prayerfully rejoiced as they saw their Roman Catholic
		and Anglo Catholic brethren making a rediscovery
			of the early forms of Holy Communion.
We have seen altars transformed into tables,
	behind which their clergy stand as those who serve
		the Guests of the Lord.
Members of the Reformed Churches rejoiced in this transformation.
They have known for centuries of experience how many and
great are the blessings of this beautifully simple form.
It is the elders in the Reformed Churches who perform
	the first action in the drama when they remove the linen
		in what is called the "unveiling of the elements."
This action is liturgically symbolic of the Christ whose flesh
	veiled the fact that he was the Lord of life.
In the minds of many people the only signs or symbols
	in our celebrations of Holy Communion
		are the elements of Bread and Wine.
These are the most obvious ones because they can be seen
	and touched.
These signs or symbols are surrounded by others
	equally meaningful, if not quite so obvious.
The late Professor P.T. Forsyth, one of Scotland's
	philosopher-theologians, reminded his fellow members
		of the Reformed Church that in the Holy Communion
			the signs or symbols consists not only of the elements
				but also of the *words spoken and the actions done*.[2]

He went on to teach that we are not to separate one of these
symbols from either of the other two.
The Early Church thought of the sacraments as a Drama
with a divine plot!
A drama that held together in harmony the words, actions, and
elements with which we are familiar.
The celebration is then something *done*,
in contrast to our emphasis on something *said*.
When the minister repeats the words of Jesus:
"Take, this is my body," we may appreciate that the act
of breaking is as significant a symbol as the bread itself.
Actually, our Reformed ancestors taught that it was in the breaking
of the bread rather than in the bread itself that the early
Christians realized the most meaningful symbol of the
crucifixion of Jesus.
The minister breaks the bread and in the fracture there is seen
all that sinful humanity does to the body of Christ.
In this breaking action, which stands so stark and clearly defined
in our Reformed worship, we glimpse the consequences of sin as the
breaking of the his body, the Church.
The same interpretation is given to the chalice of wine.
"This is my blood of the covenant," he said,
"which is poured out for many."
To you and to me,
the contents of the cup come first in symbolic importance.
The wine symbolizes the joy of his fellowship
and the bitterness of his death.
Here, again, we are reminded that to Jesus and his people,
it was the *action* of Jesus with a cup
that was most powerfully symbolic.
The outpouring of the wine in the Upper Room that evening
symbolized the actual sacrifice of his life.
Therefore, when a cup was raised no words were needed
because this was an action that took both words and breath away.
In the silence that followed,
the disciples remembered that there are some values more
precious than life itself for which a life may be given.

When the bread has been broken and the cup raised high
> in our celebrations of Holy Communion, the disciples are
>> hushed.
When they speak, it is to offer a spontaneous prayer
> of thanksgiving.
This done, the Church gathers round the Table to receive
> the elements one from the other in family fashion.
At this Table, Christ is the Head of the family and from it
> no one of his people may be excluded.
For one evening and for one evening only,
> the symbols of the Supper directed the minds of the disciples
>> to the coming Passion of their Master.
In the eventful days which followed the resurrection,
> the sacrament symbolized the presence of Christ
>> with his disciples.[3]
When the celebration in our Churches is faithful
> to the spirit of the Gospel and the intention of Jesus,
>> it points us to the Presence of Christ with his Church.
When this happens, there is forged across the centuries a link
> between the Upper Room in Jerusalem and the community
>> of Christians wherever it is you worship.
As members of the Reformed Church,
> we believe in the Real Presence of Christ in the Holy
>> Communion.
Naturally enough, we are not always sure what we mean by that.
There is a helpful illustration of what is meant
> in a lecture by Gabriel Marcel.
This is part of what he said:
> "We can have a very strong feeling that somebody who is sitting
> in the same room as ourselves, sitting quite near us, someone
> whom we can look at and listen to and whom we could
> touch if we wanted to make a final test of his reality, is
> nevertheless more distant from us than some loved one
> who is perhaps thousands of miles away, or perhaps,
> even, no longer among the living. We could say that the
> man sitting beside us was in the same room as ourselves,
> but that his presence did not make itself felt."

To that illustration we may add our own experiences!
How often have you been in a room with another person,
    and yet not with that person at all,
        except that your body was there occupying a space?
The relationship of the disciple to his Lord at the Table
    is a spiritual one, and more real on that account.
It is a more penetrating and powerful Presence than any local
    or spatial one could possibly be.[4]
What we do every time we come together to celebrate Holy
    Communion is the most wonderful thing we do upon earth.
Here, as in no other way, we proclaim the Gospel in its entirety.
Because this is true, there is no limit to our experiences of it.
In it we see love and sacrifice.
Throughout it all there is a note of jubilation.
For while we recite, as Paul says, the story of the Passion we
    we do so in the light of the life after death of our Lord.
The moment of communion is a time when words and actions,
    prayers and people come together to make the Presence of Christ
        more real to the faith of the believer than at any other time.
It will not happen again until, in obedience to Jesus,
    we meet again with one another around his Table!
        Amen.

---

1. *Letters of John Calvin* by Dr. Jules Bonnet, translated from the Latin and French languages by David Constable. Edinburgh, MDCCCLV. Vol. 2 Letter CLIX (Geneva, 17 March, 1546) fn. 75. To Theodore Vitus. ... Letter written to Calvin in response to one from him. "I have read your short address to the people on the Sacrament of the Supper, and I approve of your calling the bread and wine signs in such a sense that the things signified are in reality present. Would that they who leave only the naked signs, might be led by you."
See also John R. Donahue, S.J., David J. Harrington, S.J. *The Gospel of Mark*. (The Liturgical Press: Collegeville, Minnesota, 2002), p. 399. "In the institution narrative itself, Mark stresses the words, actions, and interpretations of the bread and wine. The bread and wine become bearers of the very presence of Jesus, which inaugurates a new covenant to be fully realized in the Kingdom of God."

2. Theodore G. Tappert, *The Lord's Supper* (Muhlenberg Press, 1961), p. 61. "Actions communicate as well as words. The question that must always be asked is: What do they communicate? The history of the Church shows that it is possible to become so preoccupied with outward forms that the *real* significance of the Lord's Supper as proclamation of the Gospel is lost sight of. ... This is what Luther meant when he declared that the Lord's Supper is a brief summary of the Gospel. Just as the oral witness not only declares something but also effects what it declares, so the action in the Sacrament not only symbolizes something but it also effects what it symbolizes."

3. Baptism, Eucharist and Ministry, Faith and Order Paper No. 14 (World Council of Churches, Geneva, 1982). "In the history of the Church there have been various attempts to understand the mystery of the real and unique presence of Christ in the Eucharist. Some are content merely to confirm the presence without seeking to explain it. Others consider it necessary to assert a change wrought by the Holy Spirit and Christ's words, in consequence of which there is no longer just ordinary bread and wine but the body and blood of Christ. Others again have developed an explanation of the real Presence which, although not claiming to exhaust the significance of the mystery, seeks to protect it from damaging interpretation."

See also a splendid review of This Order Paper by Dr. J. Robert Nelson in *The Christian Century*, September 28, 1983, pp. 546f.

4. C.K. Barrett, *Church, Ministry and Sacraments in the New Testament* (Wm. B. Eerdmans Publishing Company: Grand Rapids, Michigan, 1985), pp. 54ff.

Also Eduard Schweizer, *The Good News According to Mark*, trans, David H. Madvig (John Knox Press: Atlanta, Georgia, 1970), p. 305. "This is my body. ... the phrase means that Jesus himself will be active in the present and will confront the Church whenever it partakes of the bread and the cup."

Mark 14:12-26
1 Corinthians 5:6-8
Numbers 9:1-3, 11-12

The Farewell Meal

There are few ideas or patterns of behaviour
   that are entirely new.
Even our most original ideas have their starting point
   in an idea with which we are already familiar.
A new idea is often simply an advance on an older one.
This is true, for example, in the business world.
One marketing method or technique is replaced with a better one.
It takes place in industry
   when a new machine replaces an older one.
The principle implies that someone had enough imagination
   to see in the ideas or machines the possibilities
      for something more efficient or more cost effective.
In this instance, what is true for these areas of life
   is valid as well in the Christian religion.
Christian services of worship, in the Reformed Churches,
   began on the model of worship in the synagogue.
In the Roman Catholic and Orthodox churches,
   the services are based both on certain models
      from the Temple and the Synagogue.
The Sacrament of Baptism is patterned on the form
   once in use by Jewish people.
Converts to Judaism were baptized by immersion.
It was while they were sharing together the Passover meal
   that Jesus and his disciples shared a new experience.
It was later to be known as the Holy Communion, the Eucharist,
   the Lord's Supper, the Last Supper, or the Mass.
According to the Gospels, the words and actions of Jesus
   at that time have their roots in the past.

They were dependant for their originality
> on what Jesus understood of the future.

Jesus was a young Jewish person.
As such he never forgot his roots in the past
> and the birth of his people, Israel.

He belonged to a people whose ancestors
> had been in slavery for generations.

Bodies had been broken and minds destroyed.
Despite that reality,
> there were a few people who held stubbornly to the idea
>> that God would put an end to their cruel captivity.

Finally, there came a time when strange events and strong
> characters conspired to panic the superstitious ruler of Egypt.

In an effort to rid himself of his trouble
> the Ruler put his slave population out into the desert.

These former slaves were convinced that their good fortune
> was a part of the plan of God.

They believed that while tragedy and horror
> were allowed to come to the Egyptians,
>> they had been averted from them by the sparing hand of God.

They called the experience the "pass-over."
A religious feast was named after the momentous event.
The Feast ever afterward was known as the Passover.
Attendance at the Feast became an obligatory part of one's life.
In Jesus' home it had always been celebrated with the family.
During the meal someone told the story of the Great Escape.
The emphasis was on the fact
> that it had been masterminded and carried out by God.

The Feast of Passover was told as if it had just taken place.
Every person at the Feast was meant to feel
> that the experience had been a personal one.

Every person present had taken part in the deliverance itself.
The feeling of personal participation was created
> by the use of certain symbols and language.

Unleavened bread was used as a symbol of readiness
> in which the people waited for freedom prior to their release.

The head of the family took a piece of bread and said:
"This is the bread made ready for our deliverance."
A cup of red wine was used and of it the speaker said:
"This is the blood of the lamb that was used to sprinkle
our doorposts, so that the angel of death passed-over
our houses."
The bread and wine were not what the speaker said they were.
They represented those things.
The elements of bread and wine were signs or symbols.
As were the words used on these occasions.
Our spiritual ancestors used these signs or symbols
to represent an event in the long ago.
They used them to convey the meaning
of that event, long ago, to people in the present.
Each person at the Feast of Passover felt that he or she
had been delivered from over 6 centuries of slavery.
It was within this Passover context that Jesus spoke of himself.
In addition to the traditional words and actions at the meal
he took the unleavened bread and having broken it,
he said to the others in the room:
"Take, this is my body."
It wasn't his body, of course.
It was a sign or symbol representing his body.[1]
Even the word *body* meant more than his visible physical body.
It included as well what we would call personality or character.[2]
Jesus was using this language in the way
it was used at the Passover.
Or as it had been used by the prophets for centuries.
Think, for example, of the prophet
who took three bits of hair in his hand.
One bit he burned.
One bit he threw into the wind.
The third bit he surrounded by slashes from his sword.
When finished, he said:
"This is Jerusalem."
Which, of course, it wasn't!

It was a symbolic representation of experiences
    that would befall Jerusalem.
In the same manner, Jesus said:
    "This is my body."
At the close of the meal he took a chalice of wine and said:
    "This is my blood of the new covenant which is poured
        out for *many*."
In the Passover the wine was symbolic of the blood of an animal.
The blood that had been sprinkled on the doorposts of houses
    and, later, on the people of God.
The Passover wine was shared amongst the people.
It indicated that each person had taken part in the experience
    whereby God had rescued the people of God.
Jesus took the wine as the symbol or sign of his blood.
To the Jewish mind this meant "life" itself.
Looking into the future, and using the language of the past,
    Jesus spoke of his life to be given for all humanity.
He knew that before the week was over
    his life would be taken from him.
From a political point of view alone,
    it was an inevitable event.
This, taken with Jesus' sense of mission in carrying out
    the divine purpose for his life,
        made his expectation of death a reality.
Jesus spoke of a new covenant
    as we might speak of a Last Will And Testament.
It is not a contract between equals.
It is an inheritance from one to be shared with many.
Jesus told us that in the new covenant God will, once again,
    do something wonderful for the people of God.
The first deliverance was of a tiny nation
    from centuries of physical slavery.
This second deliverance claims as the People of God
    the whole of humanity.
The new meal was not a sort of family reunion
    based on race or language only.

Neither is it the sort of fellowship of those
    who attend weekly meetings of the local Rotary Club.
It includes all people everywhere
    and all people *equally* everywhere.
The "many people" will receive from One
    something they could not effect for themselves.
The bread and wine are signs or symbolic elements.
They re-present the life of Christ
    and its place in the plan of God.[3]
What these signs represent *for* us they also convey *to* us!
Just as they proclaim what God has done
    through the person of Christ, so they convey to us
        the presence of that person.
The signs (or symbols) of the Sacrament convey to all
    who share in them the meaning of what they represent.
It is not the bread and wine of themselves.
It is the meaning of *who* and *what* they represent
    that become a means of transforming our lives.[4]
        Amen.

---

1. John R. Donahue, S.J. & Daniel J. Harrington, S.J. *The Gospel Of Mark* (Collegeville, Minnesota: The Liturgical Press, 2002), p. 399. "In the institution narrative itself Mark stresses the words, actions, and interpretations of the bread and wine. The bread and wine become bearers of the very presence of Jesus, which inaugurates a new covenant to be fully realized in the Kingdom of God."

Dr. Jules Bonnet, *Letters Of John Calvin*. Translated from the Latin and French languages by David Constable, Edinburgh. And by Thomas Constable and Co., Little, Brown and Co., Boston, USA. MDCCCLV, Vol. 2. Letter CLIX (Geneva, March, 1546, to Theodore Vitus), fn. 75. (To the most honourable Doctor Theodore Vitus, most faithful minister of Christ at Neuremburg.) A letter written to Calvin in response to one from him. "I have read your short address to the people on the Sacrament of the Supper, and I approve of you calling the bread and wine signs in such a sense that the things signified are in reality present. Would that they who leave only the naked signs, might be led by you."

2. *Ibid.* Letter CCXXX to Henry Bullinger ... "the reality is exhibited together with the signs."

3. *Ibid* (Letter XXVIII to Farel, 24 October, 1538), p. 78. An interesting note on the celebrant of the Sacraments, a note of contemporary significance. "The sacraments are the means of communion with the Church; they must needs, therefore, be administered by the hands of pastors."

4. *Ibid* (Letter CCXXIV to Henry Bullinger, Geneva, 26 June 1848). "For with the sacraments in general, we neither bind up the grace of God with them, nor transfer to them the work of the Holy Spirit, nor constitute them the ground of the assurance of salvation. We expressly declare that it is God alone, who acts by means of the Sacraments; and we maintain that their whole efficacy is due to the Holy Spirit.... the Sacraments are instruments of the grace of God."

Mark 14:17-25
1 Corinthians 5:6-8
Numbers 9:1-3, 11-12

Memories And The Sacrament — A Meditation

There are certain experiences from our youth,
    which we never forget.
They may be buried for a time,
    and then reappear again and again
        as we grow older.
As a family in Nova Scotia,
    living on a farm, we heard the train whistle
        only on rare occasions.
When we heard it, it had a special sound.
In order to hear it, the wind
    had to be blowing in the right direction.
It was always in late autumn that we heard it.
    Just before a snowstorm.
Across the years, after I left home,
    I have heard train whistles
        in many different parts of the world.
None, however, like the one we used to hear
    when the wind was right,
        when the air was damp and chill,
            and the snow was about to begin falling.
After leaving home, and for a time,
    it seemed to me that the special sound of the train whistle
        may have been completely in my imagination.
Until one evening in Scotland, many years ago.
It was while I was spending the weekend in a cold Scottish manse
    prior to preaching on Sunday.
In the middle of the night I woke up.

At first I heard nothing at all.
Then it came — the train whistle.
The whistle blew and blew
    as the train passed through a valley
        some distance from the manse.
Then, as the train passed through the town,
    the whistle was blown again.
The next morning it snowed!
The sound of that train whistle in Forfar, Scotland,
    brought back at once many things temporarily forgotten.
The feel in the air, the chill at nightfall,
    the dead calm, and the falling snow.
The sound of the train whistle
    brought back other memories, as well.
Memories of the old farmhouse at home in Nova Scotia.
Memories of those still in it.
Memories of the oil lamps
    by which we did our homework as children.
The three-coloured cat asleep by the wood stove,
    the smell of freshly baked bread and much more.
The past was present once again.
    Time stood still.
For a little time, I was a boy again.
In a river valley in Nova Scotia,
    I saw and heard and smelled things long forgotten.
Holy Communion, the Eucharist, is something like that.
When we come here to celebrate the Sacrament
    we take hold of one end of a thread
        that goes back more than 2,000 years.[1]
On its way back, it passes through
    a lifetime of experiences for all of us.
For young people there is inevitably the memory
    of their *first* communion:
        the gleaming silver chalices,
            the plates of bread or wafers,
                the trays of glasses,
                      the presence of parents and friends.

For older people, there are memories associated with
    such celebrations going back twenty, thirty, forty, fifty,
        and even sixty years or more.
The smell of the bread and the aroma of the wine
    associate themselves at once with the words we use.
For a little time, once again we participate with our parents
    or our grandparents, or old and dear friends,
        many gone now from our sight and hearing.
We share their spirit as they waited quietly
    for the signs of Christ to come to them.
The things we see and touch and hear
    speak to us as well of the hymns they sang,
        the readings they loved,
            and the words of Holy Communion they knew by heart.[2]
Throughout it all, the past is present.
It is all as if you were actually there.
As we follow the thread back through time,
    we come eventually to the beginning of it.
There, in an Upper Room, at Passover time,
    there were memories and associations going
        back another 2,000 years, as Jesus and his disciples
            shared the last of their many meals together.[3]
The Passover things they ate together,
    the wine they shared with one another,
        the words used on that occasion were all saturated
            with the memories of the Jewish people,
                and of their special relationship with God.[4]
Whenever that meal was eaten with one another,
    the events of their salvation in the past
        were brought into the present.
They were brought into the present so realistically
    they felt they were *there* in the original experience.
At every celebration of Holy Communion,
    we bring into the present
        the events of our salvation in the past.
The Holy Communion is always our experience
    of the death and resurrection of Jesus Christ.

We are there in the large Upper Room.
We, too, hear the words, see the actions,
   smell the signs of bread and wine, and more,
     as if in the presence of Christ.
The presence of Christ with us at Holy Communion
   is as real as the presence of the person
     sitting next to you in Church this morning.
That is what we believe
   and we know it to be true!
          Amen.

---

1. Frederick C. Grant. *The Gospel According To Mark, Introduction and Exegesis. The Interpreter's Bible*, Vol. VII (New York: Abingdon Press, 1951), pp. 876-878.

2. Keith A. Matthews, *Given For You: Reclaiming Calvin's Doctrine Of The Lord's Supper* (Philippsburg, New Jersey: P&R Publishing Company, 2002), pp. 215f. "Mark alone records: 'And when they had sung a hymn, they went out to the Mount of Olives.' " This hymn was the second part of the Hallel (Psalms 114-118 or 115-118). It is interesting to note some of the words that were sung by Jesus as he prepared to go to Gethsemane and ultimately to the cross. The words of Psalm 116, for example. are a prayer of thanksgiving to God for deliverance from death and a promise to fulfil vows made to the Lord (read all of Psalm 116).

3. Dennis E. Nineham, *The Gospel Of St. Mark. The Pelican New Testament Commentaries* (New York: Penguin Books, 1963), p. 458. Reprinted many times. "In particular Mark's Gospel fails to bring out, what is probably the case, that from one point of view the Last Supper and the early Eucharists were continuations of a series of common meals Our Lord had been in the habit of holding with his disciples (and possibly with a wider circle of followers ...) which had foreshadowed and anticipated the ultimate (table) fellowship of the eagerly awaited kingdom of God."

4. Samuel Tobias Lachs, *A Rabbinic Commentary On The New Testament: The Gospels Of Matthew, Mark And Luke* (Hoboken, New Jersey: KTAV Publishing House, 1987), p. 407. "The bread is the mazah, unleavened bread. The blessing over the mazah is 'Blessed Art Thou, O Lord our God, King of the Universe, who brings forth bread from the earth.' The bread and wine are interpreted by the early Church symbolically."

Mark 15:21-32
Psalm 22:1-21

The Crucifixion

The language in this reading from Mark is remarkably restrained.
There is no attempt to create sympathy for Jesus.
There is no attempt to incite hatred toward those
    responsible for the actual crucifixion itself.
This is an event far too solemn for that sort of thing.
The facts are stated and left to stand for themselves.
There is no additional comment of any sort.
In a passage where the language is so carefully chosen,
    the reader must go through it slowly and thoughtfully.
Otherwise, we might miss what is being said.
The enemies of Jesus believed they had destroyed him.
They believed they had now seen the end of him.
Yet, according to Mark, nothing had happened that might
    have surprised anyone who had known his or her scriptures.
For all unknown, alike to the friends and enemies of Jesus,
in some mysterious way, the things they did and said
    had always been a part of the plan of God.
It is a great mystery, certainly, yet it is one the Church
believes, that in the events surrounding the death of Jesus, the
purposes of God were being fulfilled.
He was put to death beside a busy road, with two criminals.[1]
He was offered a drink of wine that had been drugged.
His clothing became the prizes in a soldiers' lottery.
While he hung on the cross,
    he was mocked and humiliated by those who passed by.
All these things about the Messiah, the Servant of God,
    a careful reader might have found in certain Psalms[2]
        and in the book of Isaiah.
It is from the perspective of those writings
    that Mark composed his Gospel.

They were proof, surely, all evidence to the contrary,
that the will of God was being fulfilled as it had been
predicted in the Hebrew scriptures.
As a part of the pre-crucifixion routine,
Jesus had been brutally beaten.
It was a procedure that brought even the strongest men
    to the edge of death.
Sometimes, even to death itself.
It is quite likely he needed the help of others to carry
the cross beam of his cross as the procession left the city
for Golgotha.
In this case, the man chosen to help him was Simon,
    a native of Cyrene.[3]
He was compelled to carry the cross beam
    in the place of another person, Simon Peter of Galilee.
We hardly need to be reminded at this point
    that Simon Peter had pledged to die with Jesus,
        if that should be necessary.
Instead of denying himself,
    taking up his cross and following after Jesus,
        he denied his Master.
Therefore, this other man, another Simon,
must do under orders what Peter had pledged to do voluntarily.
By the time this Gospel was written,
    Peter had been martyred in Rome.
Doubtless in that situation,
    he *had* carried his cross in every sense of the word.
However, on the day of the crucifixion of Jesus,
    when the disciple from Galilee ought to have done it,
        it was a native of Cyprus who carried the cross beam.
The contrast between the pledges of a disciple
    and his or her actual performance in a time of crisis
        does not end with Peter.
Earlier in the Gospel, two other of the disciples,
James and John, asked for the chief places with Jesus
when he came into his glory, into his "kingdom."

They had asked, that when the great day had come,
they might sit, one at his right hand and one at his left hand.
The places of highest honour and power
    in a secular kingdom of the day.
At the time of their impertinent request,
    Jesus had warned them:
        "You do not know what you are asking."
Neither they did!
When his royalty was demonstrated on the cross,
    Jesus had other companions with him.
In the places of James and John, his disciples,
    he had the fellowship of two robbers.
It was they who were one on his right hand and one on his left.
Just as Peter ought to have been carrying the cross beam,
    so the ambitious brothers ought to have been
        with him in his crucifixion.
However, they had harboured dreams of more comfortable places.
They had dreams of a cup brimming over with the good life,
and of a baptism into a different sort of society altogether.
It is true, though, that, like Peter,
    they were to follow Jesus later, against their will.
In the meantime, the chief places on either side of him
    were taken by two men from the city jail.
Men who were crucified were put to death where they would be seen
    by the largest number of people.
Their deaths were a warning to all who saw them
    that the Imperial power did not deal lightly
        with those who opposed it.
Jesus was put to death at a place called Golgotha,
    so named because it was shaped like a human skull.
There is a Jewish legend
    that the skull of Adam was buried at Golgotha.
In the Letter to the Church at Rome, Paul wrote
    "If through Adam's disobedience, sin, and death
    came into the world, through Jesus,
    there is obedience and life to undo Adam's wrong."[4]

The connection of Golgotha with both Adam and Jesus
    is one that Mark would have us make.
Men who were crucified were put to death
    in a location at eye-level with the travelling public.
The body of the victim was bent in an "S" shape
    to keep its feet from touching the ground.
    "The condemned were crucified naked,
    and the executioners were allowed to divide their clothing
    and property among them."[5]
As he hung dying, the crucified was frequently subjected
    to the taunts and tortures of heartless folk who saw him there
    in a completely helpless situation.
When death came with its merciful release
    from the agony on the cross, the centurion exclaimed:
    "Truly, this man was a Son of God."[6]
In his dying, Jesus was despised and rejected by passersby,
    by religious leaders in their meetings, and by those who were
        being executed along with him.
The reactions of those who watched him die
    served only to underline the complete abandonment of Jesus.
It was something that had begun long before.
The passersby were both right and wrong
    in the things they said and did to Jesus.
    "You who would destroy the Temple and build it in three days,
    save yourself and come down from the cross."
They were unable to know that in his death he was destroying
all that Temple worship had stood for in its sacrificial system.
In his dying, Jesus was replacing it with another way to God,
himself, to be raised by God from death in three days.[7]
The religious leaders, for their part, also had sport with him.
    "He saved others, himself he cannot save."
He had saved others, from their sins and diseases.
Yet, finally, in order to do as much for us,
    he could not and would not save himself.
We believe in the Son of Man today
    precisely because he did not come down from the cross.

Precisely because he did not turn his back on the plan of God,
    as he was challenged to do.
At that point the men on either side of him joined
    in the passing parade of pathetic people in their own
        outpouring of contempt and hostility toward him.
In fact, according to Mark, what they said
    was not fit even to be recorded.
The rejection and abandonment of Jesus,
    even the horror of crucifixion itself,
        have been the experiences of more people
            than we will ever know.[8]
It happens, in one form or other
    as often in our village, town, or city
        as it does in any other part of the world.
However, while this is true, and we know it is,
    what happened that morning on Golgotha was different in nature.
What happened *there*, according to the Gospels,
    was a part of the plan of God for your salvation and for mine.[9]
        Amen.

---

1. Thomas Cahill, *Desire Of The Everlasting Hills: The World Before And After Jesus* (New York: Anchor Books. A Division of Random House, Inc, 2001), p. 286. "Crucifixion was the ultimate form of Roman humiliation, and to understand it properly, we have to imagine a grove of huge poles set up on a central thoroughfare, where any day as we pass by, we may see fellow citizens pinned to poles with great iron nails, pierced through their joints, ripped open and left to be drained of blood as if they were animal carcasses."

2. Psalms 22 and 69.

3. "He never spoke a word to me,
    And yet he called my name.
    He never gave a sign to me
    And yet I knew and came."
A poem of unknown origin about Simon the Cyrenian.

4. Romans 5:19.

5. Samuel Tobias Lachs, *A Commentary On The New Testament: The Gospels Of Matthew, Mark And Luke* (Hoboken, New Jersey: KTAV Publishing House, 1987), p. 432.

6. Norman Perrin and Dennis C. Duling, *The New Testament: An Introduction*, 2nd ed. (New York: Harcourt, Brace & Jovanovich, 1982), p. 254. "The next verse (15:39) is also very important to Mark, for the centurions confession of Jesus as Son of God is the climax of Mark's christological concern. It is the first and only confession of Jesus by a human being that is not immediately corrected or reinterpreted, and the reason is that after 14:62 the reinterpretation of a confession of Jesus as Christ or Son of God by a use of Son of Man is complete, the messianic secret is finally revealed, an such a correct confession is possible."

Patrick J. Flanagan, *The Gospel Of Mark* (Manwah, New Jersey: Paulist Press, 1997), p. 164. "At last Jesus is recognized for what in truth he is, God's Son, the Beloved.... A total outsider with no knowledge of Jesus' works of power, not even of his teaching — not even a Jew, but he recognizes the Son of God. Here is the heart of Mark's message. If you want to know Jesus, if you would understand life, and understand love, if you would see true glory, if you would penetrate the mystery of God, then look at the cross — and not just Christ's cross, out there, a long time ago, but the cross borne in your life too." Many people, "succumb to the one heresy that endures in every age, the lie that pretends we can know the depths of God apart from Christ's cross."

7. The expression "three days" is meant to indicate an indeterminate length of time, as in "after a while."

8. A student at Memorial University, a veteran of the Vietnam war, was unable to deal with the Gospel accounts of the crucifixion of Jesus in a Religious Studies course on the The Life And Teaching Of Jesus. He had witnessed, with other young soldiers, the bodies of fellow American solders who had been crucified along the banks of the Mekong River.

In another sense, there are men, women, and children in our various societies who figuratively die such a death every day. Mental torture, physical abuse eventually leading to death in one of many ways, lead us to say, "She was crucified living with him."

9. Cahill, *Op. Cit.*, p. 287. "... this entire action of Jesus, of submitting to this awful suffering, was done on our behalf. We are the taunting, frightened, indifferent friends of Jesus."

Mark 16:1-8
1 Peter 1:3-9
Isaiah 25:6-9

Only The Women Were There

The Jewish Sabbath day ended at around 6 o'clock in the evening.
Afterward, the shops were free to open again.
It was an opportunity for the women to go shopping.
In this case they went looking for spices
    with which to tend to the body of Jesus.
The purpose of the spices was for the anointing.
The anointing was to keep down the stench from the corpse of Jesus.
Having obtained the spices, they went home for the night.
Very early the next morning, just as the sun was rising,
    they made their way toward the tomb.
It was the place in the rock where the body of Jesus
    had lain since Friday afternoon.
As old friends do, as they walked along the road,
    they chatted with one another in subdued tones.
Their mission was not a pleasant one.
It was made worrisome, too, by the problem of gaining
    access to the body of Jesus.
        "Who will roll away the stone for us
        from the door of the tomb?"
The entrance to the tomb was blocked by a round, flat, stone disk.
Much like the old-fashioned grindstone in shape.
Mark comments that, in this case at least,
    the stone was a large one.
It would have been very heavy.
It went down a sloping dug trench
    across the entrance of the tomb.
It would have taken several strong men
    to roll it back up the trench

in order to expose an opening.
On their way to the tomb there was no sign of men.
At one point, as they walked up the hill,
    they looked toward the tomb.
They saw then, to their astonishment,
    that the stone had been rolled away!
It was a shock to the minds and bodies of the women.
This was the first emotional shock of the morning.
Others were to follow.
When they finally got to the tomb and entered it,
    they saw what appeared to be a young man.
He was sitting at the side of the place
    where the body of Jesus had lain.
He invited the women to see for themselves
    that the grave place was empty.
It was the second emotional shock of the morning.
Once again the only witnesses were the three women.
The two Marys, and Salome.
The same three women
    who had been witnesses to the death of Jesus.
Furthermore, after the crucifixion,
    the two Marys had been witnesses to the burial of his body.
Where were the disciples?
They had disappeared.
They were now nowhere to be seen!
They had been missing for some time.
For instance, on the road to the place of crucifixion,
    Simon Peter ought to have been the person
        to carry the crossbeam for Jesus.
Instead, it was carried by another Simon,
    this one from Cyrene.
The men on either side of Jesus during the crucifixion
    ought to have been James and John.
Not knowing what they were asking,
    it was they who requested to be one on the right
        and one on the left of Jesus when he came into his glory.

Instead, their places were taken by two men from the city jail.
The disciples had disappeared
> because of their failure to be disciples.[1]

They had not really been followers of Jesus,
> much as they had appeared to follow him.

Their places had been taken by the three women.
In his death it was the women
> who had become the intimates of Jesus.

In a curious way,
> the announcement at the tomb made sense to them.

As faithful followers of Jesus,
> they knew the whole story, not only of his ministry
>> but of his ending, as well.

They were able to see in advance where it was going,
> and what the outcome was likely to be.

The writer of the Gospel of Mark
> regarded the disciples as failures.

Throughout his ministry, they had misunderstood Jesus.
They misunderstood what he taught and what he did.
The Master Teacher had to correct one misunderstanding
> after the other.

From the moment of their call into discipleship,
> they had been losers.

At the end of his ministry of teaching and healing
> according to the Gospel of Mark,
>> Jesus had been totally abandoned by his disciples.

In this Gospel,
> he had been totally abandoned by God, as well.

In this, the earliest Gospel,
> it was to three amazed, shocked, and frightened
>> women that the announcement was made.
>> "He is Risen!"

Raised by God from the dead. Incredible!
The resurrection is a breathtaking story![2]
How do you tell such a "once-ever" story?
It provided and still does provide the greatest problem in

communication in the history of the Christian Church!
Do you dramatize it in a play?
Do you compose stirring music like the "Hallelujah Chorus,"
   or one of the wonderful, triumphal Easter hymns?
Maybe all or any one of these attempts to proclaim
   something that is responsible for the existence of the Church.
Some devout Christians understand it in terms of symbolism.
For them, Easter symbolizes the triumph of Life over Death.
It symbolizes the triumph of good over evil,
   of God over Satanic influences in society.
It symbolizes, in a powerful way,
   the presence of hope in our lives.
After the first Easter, the most striking characteristic
   that distinguished Christians from their neighbours
      was their hope.
The person who looks forward to his or her Easter morning
   is not concerned with the brevity or the futility of life.
A disciple of Jesus Christ regards the end of life
   as a fresh beginning.
In that way she or he can get on with the work of the present.
The Christian hope is not a natural projection
   of human optimism.
It is a hope that this life is not all there is to living.
It is a conviction that something lies beyond the grave.
It is a conviction that our minds have been developed and our lives have been lived with an influence to persist well beyond the years we have here.
Or do you simply tell the Gospel story and leave it at that?
On Easter morning, what does it mean to you when you hear again
   that Christ was raised from the dead by God
      some 2,000 years ago?
What will it mean tomorrow morning as you go to work?
   Or relax and read the morning paper?
   Or play soccer with young friends?
It will be a different experience for each one of us.
A different life-experience depending on who or where we are.
We will live it out in our own way.

For me to say "Jesus is Risen" means many things.
It means at *least* that I experience Jesus every day
as the last word, the final word, in all things.
For me, the experience transforms the "everydayness"
of all my living and, one day, please God, of my dying!
He is Risen!³
Amen.

---

1. Norman Perrin, *The Resurrection According To Matthew, Mark And Luke* (Philadelphia: Fortress Press, 1977), pp. 31f.

2. Karl Barth, *Church Dogmatics*. "We may be Protestants or Catholics, Lutherans, or Reformed, to the right or to the left, but in some way we must have seen and heard the angels at the open and empty tomb if we are to be sure of our ground."

3. Books which were especially helpful include the following:
Jack Dean Kingsbury, *The Christology Of Mark's Gospel* (Philadelphia: Fortress Press, 1983).

Reginald H. Fuller, *The Formation Of The Resurrection Narratives* (New York: The Macmillan Company, 1971).

Gerald O'Collins, S.J., *The Resurrection Of Jesus Christ* (Valley Forge, Pennsylvania: Judson Press, 1973). Review of book by late Professor Raymond E. Brown, S.S. in *America*, June 15, 1974.

Gerald O'Collins, S.J., *The Fearful Silence Of The Three Women* (Gregorianum 69, 1988), pp. 489-503.

Norman Perrin, *The Resurrection: According To Matthew, Mark, And Luke* (Philadelphia: Fortress Press, 1997). Reviewed (not well) by Reginald H. Fuller.

W.R. Telford, *The Theology Of The Gospel Of Mark* (Cambridge, U.K.: Cambridge University Press, 2003).

Rowan Williams, *Resurrection: Interpreting The Easter Gospel* (Cleveland: The Pilgrim Press, Revised Edition, 2002).

A Basic Bibliography On The Gospel Of Mark

Kurt Aland, Matthew Black, Carlo M. Martini, Bruce M. Metzger, and Allen Wikgren, eds., Nestle-Aland 26th Edition, *The Greek New Testament*, 3rd Ed. (corrected) (New York: United Bible Societies, 1982).

Paul J. Achtemeier, *Mark, Proclamation Commentaries*, ed. Gerhard Krodel (Philadelphia: Fortress Press, 1975).

Paul J. Achtemeier, *Invitation To Mark: A Commentary On The Gospel Of Mark With Complete Text From The Jerusalem Bible* (Garden City, New York: Doubleday & Company, 1978).

Hugh Anderson, *The Gospel Of Mark, New Century Bible Commentary* (Grand Rapids, Michigan: Eerdmans, 1981).

Raymond E. Brown, S.S., *The Death Of The Messiah*, Anchor Bible Reference Library (New York: Doubleday, 1994).

Raymond E. Brown, S.S., *An Introduction To New Testament Christology* (New York/Manwah, New Jersey: Paulist Press, 1994).

John Calvin (1509-1564), *A Harmony Of The Gospels: Matthew, Mark, And Luke*, Vol. 1, Trans. The Rev. William Pringle (Grand Rapids, Michigan: Baker Book House, 1979).

C.E.B. Cranfield, *The Gospel According To St. Mark*, Cambridge Greek Testament Commentary (Cambridge, U.K.: Cambridge University Press [many reprints], 2002).

John R. Donahue, S.J. & Daniel J. Harrington, S.J., *The Gospel Of Mark* (Collegeville, Minnesota: The Liturgical Press, 2002). This is an excellent commentary.

Patrick J. Flanagan, *The Gospel Of Mark* (New York: Paulist Press, 1997).

Frederick C. Grant, *The Interpreter's Bible*, Vol. 7, Introduction and Exegesis to Mark (New York: Abingdon Press, 1951).

Jack Dean Kingsbury, *The Christology Of Mark's Gospel* (Philadelphia: Fortress Press, 1983).

Dennis E. Nineham, *Saint Mark* (New York: Penguin Books Ltd., 1979). Reprinted many times.

Eduard Schweizer, *The Good News According To Mark*, trans. Donald H. Madvig (Atlanta: John Knox Press, 1970).

W.R. Telford, *The Theology Of The Gospel Of Mark* (Cambridge, U.K.: Cambridge University Press, 1999).

Lamar Williamson, Jr., *Mark, Interpretation Series* (Atlanta: John Knox Press, 1983).